HUSH! *Listen.*

HUSH! *Listen.*

40 Days
of
"Thus Saith the Lord"

Beverly Clopton

WordCrafts Press

Hush! Listen. is dedicated to
GOD,
The Supreme Creator of
All that was; All that is; All that is to be.
To Him Be The Glory And Praise!

Contents

About This Book

I listened to the panel discussion of my book, *Lingering in the Word*, by a local church's women's ministry group, somewhat in awe of the impact it had had upon them as they studied God's word. In the following days, as my co-author, the Spirit Whisperer, and I continued to mull over both the content and context of my new manuscript, the thought emerged—*God's word feeds the soul as nothing else can.* I believe He created us to hunger for it because He knew nothing draws us closer to and aligns us with His will and purposes than the Holy Bible (our Google app for all things biblical).

In addition to engaging His word, we must accord it reverence as it is the "I Am Who I Am" speaking. The words of an old gospel choral song came to mind as how we might accomplish that.

"Hush, Hush, somebody's callin' my name.

Hush, Hush.

O my Lord, O my Lord, what shall I do?"

For believers that "somebody" is God, and what we should do when He speaks is HUSH, and LISTEN.

The word "hush" traces its etymology back to the mid-16th century as the interjection "husht" meaning "quiet." I use its verb form which simply means to "make someone be quiet or stop talking." It suggests that silence is the appropriate posture for whatever is going on in that moment. With that as its back story, HUSH! and Listen recalls the various times and situations in the Bible where the triune God and/or Jesus speak to us. These scriptures are not those written by others to advance the gospel, nor those inspired by Jesus' teachings or those who chronicled what they saw or were inspired to speak or write. This is a deeper dive into what I term "*thus says the Lord*" scriptures.

As we shut out the noise in times in which doing so is difficult, we quieten ourselves to hear "The Divine" speak words we need to hear. My hope is that in the silence of listening we grow even closer to the Trinity; that we set aside the untruths of the era and allow these Holy Words to penetrate our souls and spirits, thus equipping us to better live the faith we profess.

If you're thinking, "Umm, that's rather ambitious," I agree. But I believe it's worth the effort. What more favorable time than now to allow the spoken words of God the Father and Jesus His Son to abide in us and we in Him as disciples in a fallen world of the 21st century.

Hush. Listen. They're speaking. May we attune our ears to hear, to be haunted, to be mesmerized; and then be called to action by what they proclaim. It's listening time.

Addendum

Each devotion begins with a Holy Scripture, followed by Commentary and a Prayer. The Reflection section provides an opportunity for meditating upon what you've read and its application as you continue your spiritual journey. The Faith Response section allows space for written comments and thoughts.

HUSH!

Then God said, 'Let us make mankind in our image, in our like-ness,' … So, God created mankind in his own image, in the image of God he created them; male and female he created them.

~Genesis 1:26, 27

In the very first book of the Bible, God is not silent. He doesn't go about the task of creation muttering as a cobbler at a workbench might. No, God speaks aloud His plans for the universe as He brings them into existence. "Let there be…" is stated at each introduction of the elements that comprise the eventual structure of the earth, sky, and waters. Upon completion of each, He confirms His efforts as "good." In today's verses, God brings into the creation story His co-creator. It is a joint venture that resulted in humankind being formed in the divine image of God. God blessed the man and woman and gave purpose to their existence. His words are clear. Mankind was made in both the image and likeness of the triune God (Father, Son, and Holy Spirit).

As I reflected upon this account of creation, the import of it surfaced. God made us in His image and likeness. What exactly does that mean? What does the Bible teach us about the triune God's image and likeness? Answering this question requires a targeted dive. And it's one worth the effort when we consider the question: Do we who profess to follow Him bear His image and His likeness? Our ever-ready source—the Bible—sheds light on His image and consequentially on what that means for us who were created in it.

As we know, the term *image* generally refers to our personal identity. It is the impression we present as to who or what we are. The corresponding term *likeness* references similarity, equivalence or sameness. (Oxford Language Dictionary) God uses both terms to describe what comprises us. We might conclude it was important to Him that we understand how connected to Him we are. He wanted us to possess what He was; for our public persona to reflect His attributes. The biblical dive overflows with references to those attributes. A sampling follows:

1. *"The Lord said to Moses, … 'Be holy because I, the Lord your God, am holy.'"* (Leviticus 19:2)
2. *"God is a righteous judge…"* (Psalm 7:11)
3. *"For I, the Lord, love justice…"* Isaiah 61:8)
4. *"And he passed in front of Moses proclaiming, 'The Lord, the Lord, the compassionate and gracious God, slow to anger abounding in love and faithfulness.'"* (Exodus 34:6–7)
5. *"The Lord is merciful and gracious, slow to anger, and plenteous in mercy."* (Psalm 103:8)
6. *"Because of the Lord's great love we are not consumed, for his compassions never fail. They are new every morning."* (Lamentations 3:22–23)
7. *"But the Lord is faithful,"* (2 Thessalonians 3:3)
8. *"Jesus answered, 'I am the way and the truth and the life."* (John 14:6)
9. *"The Lord detests lying lips, but he delights in people who are trustworthy."* (Proverbs 12:22)
10. *"For God so loved the world that He gave his one and only Son, that whoever believes in him shall not perish but have eternal life."* (John 3:16)
11. *"For if you forgive other people when they sin against you, your heavenly Father will also forgive you. But if you do not forgive others their sins, your Father will not forgive your sins."* (Matthew 6:14)

In summary, our God is, among other things, holy, righteous, just, gracious, merciful, compassionate, faithful, truthful, loving, and forgiving. (Of course, because He is God, He is identified not just by those traits, but more than our human minds can express.) And if logic has any validity, we can conclude that those attributes are the ones we ought to be showcasing to the world. Right?

I'm imaging that we've arrived at a "*Come to Jesus*" moment. It's the perfect place to be as it gives us pause for reflection; to honestly examine the façades, guises, or faces we present to the world—in our personal and professional settings; our interactions; our responses to life's challenges, our reactions and countenances we project. Who or what do we emulate? What captures and holds our attention? Are we drawn more to the world's images of success and fame? Do we compare ourselves to others based upon attributes God did not include in His original design of who we are? Give the Lord His due and come into His presence with humility and honesty. God has spoken.

Prayer: Father God, I know I fall short in representing You. I too easily forget in whose image I've been saved to be like. Strengthen my resolve to reverse course and live the faith I profess. In Jesus' name. Amen.

Reflection: What resonates most with you in either the scripture or commentary or both as it relates to your spiritual journey.

Faith Response:

HUSH!

The Lord said, 'I have seen the misery of my people in Egypt. … So, I have come down to rescue them, … I am sending you to Pharoah to bring my people out of Egypt. But Moses said to God, 'Who am I that I should go to Pharoah and bring the Israelites out of Egypt? And God said, 'I will be with you.'

~Exodus 3: 7–12

The accounts of Moses, the Hebrew who was raised during his childhood and youth as the son of the Egyptian king's daughter; and the writer of the Jewish Torah and rescuer of the Israelites from slavery in Egypt are well known to Jews and Christians, as well those of other faith professions. At the time of today's scripture, Moses is said to have been in his eighth decade. He'd spent the second forty of those years as a fugitive, working as a shepherd for the father of the woman he met and married in the land to which he had escaped after he killed an Egyptian in retribution for his beating of a Hebrew slave. The conditions under which his people were living back in Egypt had gone from bad to worst since he'd left. They cried out to Jehovah and eventually God decided they'd suffered enough. He selected Moses to be His biblical "Superman" and spoke His rescue plan aloud to him. God is quite direct in what He tells Moses He wants Him to do. Interestingly, Moses seems unfazed by God's speaking directly to Him, but he balks at what he hears. His sense of "heroism" at this point measures zero. Quite bluntly, he challenges the Divine Creator. Restated, his response implies: "You have the wrong guy for that job. Who do you think

I am? No warrior here, just a humble shepherd." The Lord doesn't debate the issue; in a sense He ignores Moses' protest and moves forward with what His plans are with the simple assurance that *"I will be with you."*

Five simple words proclaim for Moses all he needs to know. Faced with a seemingly impossible charge, hesitant for all kinds of reasons (a speech disability being his best go-to), and feeling completely "out of his depth and definitely out of his lane," Moses doesn't initially get the import of God's word. He doesn't understand that though his personal toolbox may be lacking and his skill set nowhere near what the task requires, those five words have power beyond anything he can understand in the moment. And they are enough.

Nothing has changed in these thousands of years since the triune God spoke aloud those five words to Moses from a bush that didn't burn itself up. He speaks those same words to us today:

- You've been cancer free for five years, and during the sixth year, the test results suggest a recurrence. As you walk to the car, tears in your eyes, you hear God say, *"I will be with you."*
- Technological advantages finally tap you on the shoulder in the workplace, and you leave the supervisor's office with notice your position is phased out. As you ride the subway home, God says, *"I will be with you."*
- You singlehandedly balance the demands of work, home, children, and the doctor's office calls to discuss your mom's latest visit and the recommendation that she should no longer live alone as the dementia issues are worsening. You hang up the phone, overwhelmed, and you hear God say, *"I will be with you."*
- The morning dawns and as you open your eyes to the new day, immediately you're aware that the challenges you fell asleep with haven't disappeared. No, they crowd your mind, signaling for despair to join the party. And in that moment, you remember the prayers you prayed before you fell asleep, and God says, "I *will be with you.*"

Oh, the scenarios of the times in which we live, desperate for rescue, for help, for healing, for a way out of a no-way out situation are seen by God as surely as He saw them in biblical times. We find hope in the reality that Jesus our Savior continues to advocate and intercede for us in this fallen world. And even as we like the Hebrew slaves still cry out against oppression and oppressors, the triune God hears. In his timing, His will for His people will prevail. Stay in His word. Attune your ear, heart, and mind to hear Him in those critical moments. Those five words are eternal. We know because He said them aloud. Like Moses, we must accept what He says and in faith move as He so calls. Hush! He is with you.

Prayer: Father God, I confess that too often in the initial moments of adversity, I forget your promise. Help me to mature in faith such that when my world is turned upside down, my first response will be simply, "God is with me."

Reflection: What resonates most with you in either the scripture or commentary or both as it relates to your spiritual journey.

Faith Response:

HUSH!

The Lord answered Moses, 'Is the Lord's arm too short? You will now see whether what I say will come true for you.'"

~Numbers 11:23

As the Israelites' journey to the promised land continued, so did their complaining. The manna, i.e. bread, God provided was not enough for them. "*We were better off in Egypt!*" they wailed. They wanted meat! Poor Moses was at his wit's end as we say and complained to the Almighty that this leadership of His people was more than he could bear alone. He needed help. God's response didn't exactly sound like a workable solution, and Moses' exasperation with what God proposed prompted the rhetorical question. It was intended to remind Moses who God is.

James Weldon Johnson, in his novel *The Autobiography of an Ex-Colored Man*, used the phrase, "*Your arm's too short to box with God.*" That adaptation of the Lord's answer in his conversation with Moses still holds sway. God's arm represents His power. It was at this juncture of the ancient freedom march that God reminded His people: My arm was long (powerful) enough to bring you out of bondage in Egypt. It was long (powerful) enough to make a highway through a river by holding its waters as walls lining your path as you walked through to dry land. It was long (powerful) enough to provide bread for your tables. And you question now whether I'm able to do what I said I will do. Come on, Moses, your arm's too short to box with Me. You need to leave doubt at the door when you come into My Presence. Nothing is too hard for me.

It's day five of the second month of the year 2025 as I pen these words. Whereas the beginning of a new year typically symbolizes for many the opportunity for a fresh start, so far that doesn't seem to be the case. With a radical change in the nation's leadership at the federal level, the continual journey to be who we say we are, "one nation under God, indivisible, with liberty and justice for all," appears stymied and in too many instances blocked by "ism" walls and other obstacles that invalidate that identity. Irrespective of race, age, gender, or any of the other self-identifiers we've given ourselves in modern times, we feel our brother Moses' frustration and exasperation. At the city, the town, the state, the nation and international levels, we are sinking beyond our depth in finding solutions to the problems that stare us in the face. We echo Moses' plea—we can't do this alone. We need help. We need somebody to hold back the waters of indifference toward the least, the last, the lost, the widowed, the orphans, the unsheltered, the refugee, the victimized, the undereducated, the incarcerated, the young, the aged; we need help to navigate the wildernesses of poverty, homelessness, crime in the streets and in boardroom, the technology gone amok, war, greed, arrogance, inequality, and justice denied.

I submit we are at a similar moment on our journey to the Promised Land (Eternity) as were Moses and God's people at the juncture of their journey noted in the scriptures. Both spiritual and secular leaders, and we the people who have confessed Christ as our Savior must cease our whining about and lamenting the conditions of the moment. Now is the time for us to lean into our faith in both profession and practice. Now is the time to draw nearer to God through the study of His word and in continuous prayer so that we are equipped to challenge the enemy intent upon undermining God's purposes. But most importantly, now is the time to let God be God. To believe that nothing is too difficult for Him, that whatever He allows has His purpose embedded within it. Now is the time to be thankful that His arm—His power—is supreme. Those who think they're running things can lace on their gloves and step into the ring to challenge His sovereignty if they dare to. But be assured; God's question to Moses resonates down through time. Hush! Hear

Him today as He speaks to us: "Is the Lord's arm too short?" We can respond, *"No, it's not."* He proved it thousands of years ago, not inside a ring, but on a wooden cross. The "Somebody" we say we need has already delivered the winning punch. The power of His arm proved enough then; it will now and always.

Addendum: At this moment in our history, it seems many of the structures and beliefs that have defined us as a nation are under attack. We are more a "Divided States" than a "United States" of America. Reflect upon God's word to Moses who was frustrated and seemingly at a loss at that time in their story. Should we accept God at His word, and trust that His "arm" is sufficiently long enough for the challenges we face today?

Prayer: Father God, in all honesty, we confess the headlines often cast a pall of doom. In those moments when we're tempted to give into despair, help us to draw upon our faith and sure knowledge of who you are; that no challenge is too big for the God who created everything. In Jesus' name, Amen.

Reflection: What resonates most with you in either the scripture or commentary or both as it relates to your spiritual journey.

Faith Response:

HUSH!

"As I was with Moses, so I will be with you; I will never leave you nor forsake you. … Do not let this Book of the Law depart from your mouth; meditate on it day and night, so that you may be careful to do everything written in it. …Be strong and courageous. Do not be afraid, do not be discouraged, for the Lord your God will be with you wherever you go."

~Joshua 1:5; 8a; 9b

For forty years, the Israelites had wandered in the wilderness led by their patriarch Moses. At the time of the conversation noted in the chapter scriptures, God is speaking to Joshua following Moses' death. The mantle of leadership has passed to the apprentice. Note that God's first comments are words of encouragement and faithfulness. The Lord will honor the promises He made to Abraham and his progeny. He assures Joshua that the relationship He had with Moses He now transfers to Him, the new leader of His people. He then reminds Joshua of the importance of the Book of the Law He'd given to Moses; that obedience to it must continue and would be accomplished through meditation and reflection. And finally, God instructs Joshua to be neither discouraged nor fearful of the journey's challenges they would face. God would not forsake them; indeed, He would accompany them wherever they went. In the following verses of this first chapter of the Book of Joshua, the new leader is quick to obey God's word. He shared with his countrymen all the Lord proclaimed to him.

It was a "Hush" moment as the Israelites listened to what "thus says the Lord." Though they had not been in His immediate presence when God "held the mike" and proclaimed the words above, it did not alter the reality that He spoke. And His words were important. They were divine promises that would ensure their conquest of the land and the fulfillment of the Lord's purposes.

The words God spoke to Joshua He speaks to all who will hear Him today, in this space and this time. As it was for those Israelites it is for us, a "Hush" moment. In reverence and silence, we hear Him speak:

- *"So do not fear, for I am with you; do not be dismayed, for I am your God. I will strengthen you and help you. I will uphold you with my righteous right hand."* (Isaiah 47:10)
- *"When you pass through the waters, I will be with you; ... when you walk through fire you shall not be burned; the flames shall not set you ablaze."* (Isaiah 43:2)
- *"For I know the plans I have for you"* declares the Lord, *"plans to prosper you and not to harm you, plans to give you hope and a future. Then you will call on me and come and pray to me, and I will listen to you."* (Jeremiah 29:11–12)
- *"Give ear and come to me; listen, that you may live. ...Seek the Lord while he may be found, call on him while he is near. ... For my thoughts are not your thoughts, neither are my ways your ways,"* declares the Lord, *"so is my word that goes out from my mouth; it will not return to me empty but will achieve the purpose for which I sent it."* (Isaiah 55:3, 6, 8, and 11)

The Lord's divine instructional manual, our Holy Bible, is the written format of the bedrock of our faith. His words were spoken to be heard then and now, and not just in worship service when the pastor asks us to open our Bibles as he reads a passage selected for the morning's sermon. No, our triune God intended His words to echo in every facet of our life. Because we believe those words were spoken in perpetuity, we are called to turn to them as did our biblical forerunners. Currently, we live in an era captured as follows in paraphrase in the opening lines of the classic novel, A Tale of Two Cities (Charles Dickens): It was *"the best of times, the worst of times;* *"the age of wisdom, the age of foolishness; the season of light, the season of darkness; the spring of hope, the winter of despair."* From one perspective, many of our secular advances in science and technology, education and health are signs that this is *"the best of times."* Yet juxtaposed alongside them are our glaring failures: homelessness, undereducated young people leaving school ill-prepared for the demands of the world in which they must function, mounting mental health issues that challenge the fabrics of families and communities, and cultural, social, and political divisiveness that suggest this also is *"the worst of times."*

Given these realities, the question for believers is a no-brainer. What strategies do we employ in "times" like these to continue in faith? First and foremost, we get quiet and "Hush." We listen, as the psalmist reminds us in Psalm 121 who this God is that we're listening to. He is the Lord, the maker of heaven and earth. As the scriptures above confirm, He has spoken. Irrespective of how dismal, how frightening, how baffling, how seemingly unsolvable, how divisive, how insane times appear, we are not to be afraid. We are not to cower. We are not to sink into depression or apathy. We are not to lose hope, nor question whether God can handle what appears to be the collapse of a nation. God tells us clearly what we are to do. Hear Him in His continuing words noted in Jeremiah 29:12–14. The Lord speaks, *"Then you will call on me and I will listen to you. You will seek me and find me when you seek me with all your heart. I will be found by you, declares the Lord, and bring you back from captivity."* Quietly, we process His words and realize that *"there is a balm in Gilead."* The God who speaks through His word will bring us back from captivity to the perils of the moment when we understand and act upon the prerequisite He laid out—seeking Him with our all our heart. Or as He proclaimed in 2 Chronicles 7:14: *"if my people who are called by my name will humble themselves and pray and seek my face and turn from their wicked ways, then I will hear from heaven and I will forgive their sin and will heal their land."*

I don't think God can be any clearer. He promises to be with us through thick and thin times; He desires us to listen as through His words He speaks and be obedient to what He commands; He tells us to not be afraid because He will never leave us to handle life on our own when we seek and obey Him. The quietness of the moment lingers. The mike drops.

Prayer: Father God, in the stillness of the moment in which we realize that your holy word contains your promises, and that those promises are eternal, may we find the courage to press on, to stay the course. We know You will never fail. In Jesus' name, Amen.

Reflection: What resonates most with you in either the scripture or commentary or both as it relates to your spiritual journey.

Faith Response:

HUSH!

But the Lord said to Samuel, 'Do not consider his appearance or his height, for I have rejected him. The Lord does not look at the things people look at. People look at the outward appearance, but the Lord looks at the heart.'

~I Samuel 16:7

In the verses preceding the chapter verse, God had instructed the prophet Samuel to go to Bethlehem to the home of Jesse, who had a son God had chosen to become the next king of Israel. As the sons arrive, Samuel declares, "*Surely the Lord's anointed stands here before the Lord.*" It is at that moment that God speaks the chapter verse. On the contrary none of the seemingly perfect candidates passing before him "fit the bill." Though from outward appearances they seemed just the sort of individual the Lord would want, they didn't pass God's "heart" exam. God is unconcerned with what we look like, nor does He take stock of the usual measurements of a human heart—heart rate, blood pressure, rhythm and sounds of the heart valves—that determine cardiac function. No, His heart exam is targeted to that which reveals who a person is on the inside. That's his measuring stick.

I had selected this scripture of God at the mic several days before a doctor's appointment. As I neared the parking exit station, I rolled down my window with payment in hand for the attendant. Surprisingly, he shook his head from side to side and said, "*You don't have to pay. Just go.*" The barrier arm started to rise, and I exclaimed, "*What? Why?*" With a smile, he answered, "*It's Pretty Lady Day. You're a pretty lady, so it's free. Just go ahead.*" To say I was dumbfounded doesn't begin to capture the moment. I managed to say, "*Thank you*" before hurriedly driving onto the street, a big smile plastered on my face. Of course, my next thought was "Favor. God's favor!" I couldn't wait to call my sisters and share the experience. Proudly, I proclaimed, "It's Pretty Lady Day, and I passed the test." It was a merriment moment.

As I began the chapter commentary, I thought about that experience. There's no way to know what prompted the parking lot attendant to show me favor that day. If it was my appearance, so be it. But the reality is that how I look physically has little to do with who I am. Who I am is revealed within me, a function of my heart. Even on "Pretty Lady Day." It was the same in that moment that God took the mic and spoke to Samuel. He needed the prophet to understand that the eyes may see promise, but only the heart reveals the truth of a matter. We might say Samuel, in that moment, had succumbed to the lyrics of the 1973 song by the Dramatics, "*What You See is What You Get*." In other words, what the eye beholds is the essence of that person. Perhaps in the sons who paraded before him, Samuel saw the bearing, the physical attractiveness or strength he thought a king should possess. But the Gershwin brothers' song in the opera *Porgy and Bess* reminds us, "*It Ain't Necessarily So*." Our façades or public personas are not necessarily who we are. To the contrary. Only the heart reveals that. It is God's identification marker. So, what attributes of the heart was God looking for in this to be anointed king? Take a seat and allow his Holy Word to remind you.

- Proverbs 15:14–16 *"The discerning heart seeks knowledge, … the cheerful heart has a continual feast."*
- Matthew 15:18–19 *"But the things that come out of a person's mouth come from the heart, and these defile them. For out of the heart come evil thoughts—murder, adultery, sexual immorality, theft, false testimony, slander."*
- Matthew 9:4 *"Knowing their thought, Jesus said, 'Why do you entertain evil in your hearts?'"*
- I Chronicles 28:9 *"… for the Lord searches every heart and understands every heart and every thought."*
- Proverbs 4:23 *"Above all else, guard your heart, for everything you do flows from it."*

- Psalm 139:23 *"Search me, God, and know my heart; test me and know my anxious thoughts."*

God is clear. He looks at the heart to confirm that irrespective of outward appearances, a person has the traits He deems worthy—a heart that is discerning, cheerful, absent of the evil thoughts as noted above; a heart open to inspection by Him; and a heart mindful that what flows from it defines the person from which it comes. In other words, God is looking for hearts that can pass His heart exam and function according to His purposes.

Less important than that which the world espies when it glances your way or even lingers in wonderment at what it sees is the condition of your heart that the Lord's divine stethoscope monitors constantly,

He wants the world to stare at someone with a heart that pleases and honors Him, a future runway walker in Heaven, sporting a heart full of His glory.

Prayer: Father God, give me this day a heart more like yours. In the areas in which it is not, cleanse it until it gleams with your spirit. In Jesus' name I pray. Amen.

Reflection: What resonates most with you in either the scripture or commentary or both as it relates to your spiritual journey.

Faith Response:

HUSH!

"Come now and let us reason together," says the Lord. "Though your sins are like scarlet, they shall be white as snow; though they are red like crimson, they shall be as wool. If you are willing and obedient, you will eat the good of the land. But if you refuse and rebel, you shall be devoured by the sword, for the mouth of the Lord has spoken."

~Isaiah 1:18–20 NKJV

Among the books of the Old Testament, Isaiah is the second most quoted in the New Testament; the Book of Psalms is first. It begins the prophetic period in which God speaks to and through those whom He had called to proclaim His word and judgment. The chapter verses above begin Isaiah's vision concerning Judah and Jerusalem thought to be written between 745 and 680 B.C. I recalled a similar expression voiced by the main character, Vito Corleone in the book and movie *The Godfather*: "I came here to reason together." It was an invitation to those with whom he was in dispute to engage in conversation to resolve their differences. In the world in which the Corleone family operated, differences could be worked out between equals.

Upon first reading of the verses above we might conclude that God was doing the same. He was not. In the world in which we live, that is far from the case. We are not God's equal and cannot negotiate with Him. There is no negotiating sin. Either we obey His word, or we don't. And when we don't, His Presence fills both the bench and the jury box. In Isaiah's vision, He voiced the transgressions of

His people—sinfulness and disobedience. Because He is a forgiving God, He offered them a way forward—a willingness to change; and He concluded by identifying the consequences if they refused His offer. He had spoken.

Little has changed since the prophet penned those words to a wayward people. They carry the same weight for us today. As our biblical ancestors, we are weighed now by sin; resistant to obedience; and masterful at negotiating or justifying our transgressions. We tweak the Word to conform to our sinful practices. We massage the messages of the prophets, of Jesus Himself and those He sent forth to share His teachings throughout the world. We live in a time in which "reason" is a definer of who we are. We reason with, reason against. We embrace "no earthly reason," or "listening to reason." The Creator of everything including the word "reason" brings to the usage of the word His Sovereignty. In that sovereignty is His definition. His evidence in the case against us. We stand accused and rightfully so. And lest we suffer the fate of the those He accused and found guilty many eons ago, may we hear His words as if He stands at the mic proclaiming them now.

Prayer: Father God, our resemblance to your people of old feels us with dread. We favor them too much. In this moment, we acknowledge this likeness in our thoughts, words and deeds. Forgive us and guide our feet back onto the path to eternity. In Jesus' name. Amen.

Reflection: What resonates most with you in either the scripture or commentary or both as it relates to your spiritual journey.

Faith Response:

HUSH!

This is what the Sovereign Lord, the Holy One of Israel says, "In repentance and rest is your salvation, in quietness and trust is your strength, but you would have none of it."'

~Isaiah 30:15

In the saga of God's prophet Isaiah, today's verse highlights a divine proclamation during the reign of King Hezekiah, considered one of the more obedient kings of Judah. God's word, spoken via the prophet's vision is yet another moment for us to Hush. It is a verse of warning for the king and the people. Their toying with the idea of seeking help from the Egyptians in their conflict with the Assyrians, God declares, will not save them from God's ultimate plans for the nation. Despite God's ongoing admonitions to them regarding their behaviors and attitudes, the people persisted in defying God's commandments and laws. At this point, they chose instead to place their trust elsewhere.

Rather than turning from their sins in repentance and waiting on God for their salvation, they placed their bets on a nation that didn't even believe in their God. Forfeiting the strength that only God could give, they forewent their trust in Him, seemingly forgetting how He had delivered them time and again in the past. At that juncture, God picked up the mic.

Isaiah 30:15 is a simple verse really; one as well suited for them in that historical period as is its applicability to us in the twenty-first century. Yet again, God's word solidifies its eternal relevance. The elementary reality is that though outwardly our lives bear little resemblance to our distant biblical ancestors, inwardly we are like identical twins. As such we, like them, have set aside the disciplines of faith (praying, studying His word, silent times of reflection, and waiting on Him in trust), that we embraced when we first committed our lives to Him. In one breath, we call Him Lord, and in another invalidate that declaration by elevating something secular as an answer to the challenges of our times. In the year of the Lord 2025, easy access, quick solutions, and things with no long-term track record of deliverance have become the gods we worship and hail as solutions. Such practices are akin to a "slap in the face" to the God of creation and Giver of our salvation. Those simple words the Sovereign Lord spoke then He declares to us now. Oh, that we may have the wisdom to hear Him and to act upon what He says before He allows us to suffer the consequences of ignoring Him. May we repent of those attitudes and behaviors that don't line up with His word. May we learn to rest in the truth of them and there know the salvation of Christ's sacrifice on the cross for our sins. May such a renewal of the vows we took when we accepted Jesus as Lord of our lives revitalize and elevate our trust in Him as we live in a fallen world fraught with troublesome issues. And perhaps then, what He said to the people of Judah He will not need to proclaim to us. Instead, we will have all of what they missed—salvation and strength to live lives of obedience, worship and praise to the one and only God.

Prayer: Father God, you don't puzzle us with SAT words or expressions that make us scratch our heads. Instead, you speak simple, everyday words filled with the power to turn us away from sin to salvation. Give us ears to hear and hearts to obey so that we receive what you have for us. Save us from us. In Jesus' name. Amen.

Reflection: What resonates most with you in either the scripture or commentary or both as it relates to your spiritual journey.

Faith Response:

HUSH!

*"I the Lord do not change. … Ever since the time of your ancestors
you have turned away from my decrees and have not kept them.
Return to me, and I will return to you, says the Lord."*

~Malachi 3:6–7

The immutable God picks up the mic once more in a dialogue with
the prophet Malachi. His message was for the Israelites, especially
those who had returned from captivity in Babylon. In its entirety,
this final book of the Old Testament is considered a prophetic book
of judgment rather than deliverance. God's words in the chapter
verses are blunt. He is the immutable God who had not changed
over the course of His relationship with the people He proclaimed
as His own. Time and time again, He had demonstrated His care
and love for them. Yet despite all He'd done on their behalf, they
failed to obey the laws and commandments He had set before them.
Further reading of this four-chapter book reveals the ways in which
God called them out: blemished sacrifices, priestly waywardness,
and robbing God in their tithes and offerings. The Almighty God
threw down the gauntlet so to speak. He was who He said He was,
the unchanging God. It was decision time for the people.

Approximately 2,425 years have elapsed between the time in which
Malachi penned this book, and our current year 2025 AD. During
that span, God's immutability was restated by others. The psalmist
wrote in Psalm 102:25–27: *"God will not perish but will remain. His
years have no end."* The prophet Isaiah declared, *"The Lord is the
everlasting God."* The overarching theme of the Lord's unchanging

nature didn't end with the Old Testament. As the New Testament writings confirm, it carried over as divine authority for the people who followed Jehovah. To seal the permanency of His covenant, God sent His Son Jesus in what might be termed a last-ditch effort to provide a way for the people to return to Him, so that He could reciprocate, and return to them.

God's discourse with Malachi has not lost its import; it holds sway now. The writer of Hebrews avows *"Jesus Christ is the same yesterday and today and tomorrow."* (13:8) *"Because God wanted to make the unchanging* (immutable) *nature of his purpose very clear to the heirs of what was promised* (all who believed in and accepted Jesus Christ as His Son and their savior), *he confirmed it with an oath."* (6:17) (addition mine) At this writing, we are in the middle of the third month of 2025. Without doubt it is an evolving era when many of the norms that define us as a nation are rapidly changing. The English idiom, *"Don't throw the baby out with the bathwater,"* is an apt descriptor of what we are experiencing. At all levels of governance, those in positions of authority seem determined to eliminate what we've embraced for decades as valuable for the welfare of our nation—equality, inclusion, diversity, justice, free speech, (in essence our Bill of Rights)—in a rush to eliminate what they've decided are unwanted or unnecessary. From the secular perspective, the times indeed are "a changing." But praise be to God, there is more to life than just what we perceive with our eyes and hear with our ears. There is the secular and there is God, who created the secular to serve his purposes. What do we say in days like this? Has God changed? Is He no longer the God of yesterday, today and tomorrow, the God of eternity? What silly questions! Of course He has not changed. His words do not change. He's doing what He said when He talked with Malachi. He's waiting on us to return to Him; and then He will return to us. In the meantime, we who follow Jesus and believe in God as the final authority on earth and in Heaven keep on keeping the faith. We engage as He so leads us to in challenging those threats to time-honored policies that are sanctioned by God for His people in this space and time. We are not silenced in speaking truth by fear of retaliation. God is our hope and our protection in times of trouble, times such as these.

Prayer: Father God, the times are changing but we know You are not. Stand with us in this season of upheaval. Give us your strength as we give You our hearts and are obedient to Your will. In Jesus' name we pray. Amen.

Reflection: What resonates most with you in either the scripture or commentary or both as it relates to your spiritual journey.

Faith Response:

HUSH!

"For I desire mercy, not sacrifice, and acknowledgment of God rather than burnt offerings."

~Hosea 6:6

The story of the prophet Hosea is a hard one to wrap our minds around in the culture of our times. God purposely called him to marry someone who would be unfaithful to him; and would continue to do so even after his repeated efforts to bring her back into the marriage covenant. His attempts to salvage their relationship were heroic. Few if any contemporary marriages survive repeated infidelity by either party. Divorce lawyers and courts are such a common part of society that no one blinks an eye when brides and grooms who've repeated vows to one another end up employing their services.

It helps to view the book as an allegory that juxtaposes the strained relationship of Hosea and his wife Gomer with that of God and the Israelites of the northern kingdom and the people of God everywhere. Its import for believers today is as it was for those of our biblical ancestors. God desires us, His people, to live within the covenant we agreed to when we professed our belief and faith in Him and accepted Jesus as Lord of our lives. Inherent in that covenant relationship are God's expectations of how we live with one other and most importantly in our obedience to His commands and teachings.

At the time of this divine rebuke, His people had forgotten that their covenant with God represented more than just the religious rituals they observed. In effect they had massaged the spirit of the covenant such that it lost its purpose: love of God and obedience to

Him. Caught up in adherence to the law's requirements of sacrificial burnt offerings, they lost sight of who God was and who they were in relationship to Him. What God desired was their hearts, for He knew that it is from there mercy flows, worship of Him begins, and obedience follows.

Honest reflection on our part reveals that times haven't changed all that much. We have become experts in the "ritual-ology" of our faith. Not even considering the multiplicity of our denominational affiliations, each with its own dogmas, a plethora of rituals dot the landscape of the church today. Worship styles vary and people find their niche. Yet within the diversity that comes with "different strokes for different folks," a key question hoovers for us individually and collectively: "Why do we worship?" Because that's what we grew up doing; what others in our social group do; because we want to hedge our bet on this "heaven and hell" construct, because our mate goes, because we "kinda sorta" understand what it means but we're not sure, so we go hoping to one day get it. God desires our worship for the reason He desired it when He created us. He wants our heart, the essence of our being, the part of us that is part of Him and that's what real worship is. Giving our heart to God; and in so doing demonstrating our love of Him via our obedience to His commands. Yes, our offerings, our tithes, and our service are needed, but they're more the side dishes on our faith menu. The entrée is what God Himself declares as so written by the prophet Micah: *"And what does the Lord require of you? To act justly and to love mercy and to walk humbly with your God."* Micah 6:8

Such are the times in this fourth month of 2025 AD that these words of God resonate with acute urgency. He calls us to worship Him not just in a sanctuary on a particular day of the week, but rather by acknowledging His sovereignty as Lord of all and to live with mercy extended to others. To let the rituals of our faith take a backseat to the two desires He spoke then and that echo still today.

Prayer: Father God, forgive us for being comfortable with form, and ignoring substance in our worship of You. Guide us back to what You spoke so many ages ago. Instill in us the desires of your heart that we might turn from empty worship and mockery of your words. We cannot do it alone, Father. In Jesus' name. Amen.

Reflection: Examine your faith practices for "empty worship" or anything that bypasses as faith as understood in today's scripture. What steps do you need to take to turn away from them?

Faith Response:

HUSH!

"For I know the plans I have for you, declares the Lord, plans to prosper you and not harm you, plans to give you hope and a future."
~Jeremiah 29:11

God spoke this familiar verse to the Israelites during one of their darkest periods. As they began their exile in Babylon following the invasion of their country, God told them through the prophet to settle down and get on with their lives despite the circumstances. Further, God proclaimed that after seventy years, He would take them back home. Though scholars vary in their opinions regarding the actual length of time that passed before the captives returned, most agree the exile lasted a significant number of years. As the scriptures read, the people commenced to build homes, work, marry and have children while seeking also to reside peacefully and prosper in that foreign land. They trusted God would do what He'd spoken through the prophet.

As noted, the chapter scripture is quite familiar. It's one of those Bible verses captured on caps, cups, plaques, calendars, wrist bands, pendants, baby paraphernalia, graduation cards, etc. To believers and even non-believers, it speaks to the human need for a hope-filled future; one that provides opportunities for prosperity and peace. The Lord's declaration that He knows us, and that He has plans for our wellbeing in times of celebration and most especially during the not-so-good seasons when life is turned upside down. Believing that we serve and worship this God who is sovereign, who knows the future because He creates it, who designs the trajectory of our life story to satisfy His purpose and plan gives us hope and freedom from needless worry.

This does not mean however that we will avoid life's trials and tribulations. After all, the Israelites still endured seventy years of captivity. Today, we live in a fallen, sinful world. As "captives" of it we will face and endure its inherent hardships. And as has been stated, God did not create human robots, but rather people with free-will. In our natural state, we bear the consequences of our decisions and actions. Yet, even as do, we have God's word that He will not abandon us (as He did not the Israelite captives) but will shepherd us during the "going-through" times. For the future that He promises is not limited by time or space. God's future is beyond what is seen with the natural eye. And though the ancients looked for just a return and rebuilding of their earthly country one day, we contemporary followers of the one and only God know there is more to the promise of the verse. The Lord's promise and plan for us is a future with Him eternally. Where we are is just temporary, what we have is just temporary, who we are is just temporary. The day is forthcoming (and soon I hope) when God's ultimate plan will shatter the heavens and usher in eternity, our everlasting future.

Prayer: Father God, as "captive" sojourns in this temporary place, continue to guide our steps and to direct our planning. Help us live purpose-filled lives that bring good to others and glorify You. In Jesus' name. Amen.

Reflection: Meditate upon the notion that we are "captives" in a land waiting to go home. Did the commentary bring new insights or confirm the ones you already had. Respond in the space provided below.

Faith Response:

HUSH!

"You will seek me and find me when you seek me with all your heart."
~Jermiah 29:13

Chapter eleven's scripture is a concluding message of God's encouragement. It followed the words He had spoken in the previous chapter. He desired the people to understand that the promises He had spoken aligned with their actions. Their past behaviors had led to their current circumstances. The ball was now in their court; it would be incumbent upon them to find their way back to the Lord, or as might be said in contemporary usage "to get back in His good graces." The road to that end required "seeking" Him, and that would entail being obedient to the laws and commandments within the covenant He had established. The time for half-hearted, cursory actions was long past.

Interestingly, these words of our Lord have as much meaning for us today as they did for those captive Israelites. Though we aren't physically captive in the country in which we reside, many of our behaviors suggest that our hearts are. The very place that is the mirror of our soul and reflects our desires is often the place that seeks the world's pleasures rather than the Lord. We reject the freedom of the cross and bow in captivity to the secular.

Think for a moment of the ease with which we live as secular captives all the while claiming to profess Christ. In the ordinary coming and going of our lives, our faith is not usually what the world first espies. If no snags, no immediate or acute issues have tapped us on the shoulder, Faith waits in the recess of our consciousness. God's plans are unsolicited as the attractions of the secular beckon, and in a myriad of disguises, "Fame" and "Fortune," captivate. The allegiance to God we've claimed weakens and when not totally abandoned, assumes a dual nature. We master the categorization of the sacred and the secular; and in due time believe that such dualism is the norm. We sing and shout our love for Him at Sunday worship services (or Saturday as is the practice of some Christian churches) and use His name in vain on Monday morning as the drive to work in standstill traffic tries our patience. During our waking hours, time in His presence via His word and prayer lessens and "seeking" Him as He proclaimed moves further down on the day's list of "must dos."

What we must understand is that God's command is crucial to living in ways that allow us to live in right relationship with Him. It's on us to cast out and to refrain from all behaviors that are contrary to His standards. In so doing we reap the benefits of His grace and favor. We come truly to know Him as our God when we obey Him. He has told us what He wants. We must choose: Being held in the grip of secular captivity or flourishing in the joy of the sacred.

"Choose this day whom you will serve." Joshua 24:15

Prayer: Father God, what you ask of us doesn't require an advance degree in theology. You ask simply that we seek you with our whole hearts. Help us in the struggle to do that; to forego our self-imposed captivity after Christ has already set us free; to be an obedient people whose hearts belong to you alone. In Jesus' name we pray. Amen.

Faith Reflection: Do you enjoy the freedom Christ has afforded you or are you still struggling in captivity in the secular world's temptations? Set aside time to do some serious reflection. Respond in the space provided.

Faith Response:

HUSH!

*"You are the light of the world. … let your light shine before others,
that they may see your good deeds and glorify your Father in heaven."*
~Matthew 5:14, 16b

After His baptism and 40 days spent in the wilderness being tempted by the devil, Jesus began His ministry in earnest. Though His intent in what's known as "The Sermon on the Mount" was to teach His disciples the "constitution of faith," of what it meant to be a believer, it spoke also to all who had ears to hear what the kingdom of God is like. And though it may not have been His intention, the "teach-in" drew a crowd. Chapters five, six, and seven of the Gospel of Matthew comprise the sermon. Gems of divine wisdom are sprinkled throughout; words of the Son layered with meaning for us today.

If you went to Sunday School or Vacation Bible School as a child, you'll have no problem recalling the lyrics, "This little light of mine, I'm gonna let it shine," that you sang, often holding a candle as you and the others followed the teacher's waving arms of choral directing. A simple song, "This Little Light of Mine," is a traditional gospel hymn written for children and a wonderful musical interpretation of Jesus' message spoken so long ago. Its words remain today a reminder of who we are and what our identity as Christ followers ought to look like. The Savior's characterization of His disciples as "light" places them and us within the grandeur of the heavenly realms when we recall that God created light through the formation of the sun and moon, celestial forms to dispel the darkness that covered the earth. Our acceptance of God's grace and our vow to follow Him require us to do pretty much the same, to bring light into the dark spaces and seasons where we are.

We activate this proclamation of Jesus by first acknowledging that the "how to" of what we are called to do—"let your light shine before others"—does not require extensive research or long-drawn-out committee meetings to arrive at the best strategical approaches. No, "light shining" is summed up already in the persona of the Light Giver Himself. As He was during His sojourn on earth in His relationships and interactions with others, so we are called to be. What we do and speak, and how we live illuminate who we are. When the light we shine is His light, we dispel darkness in some of its more common guises: despair, depression, sadness, grief, fear, anxiety, worry. Instead, we shine our light in ways that please and honor God. We become more intentional in showing kindness and compassion to those in need; lending a hand and when possible, a way up and out of the darkness; opting to treat others as we want them to treat us; shunning pride for humility, refusing to allow life's challenges to steal our trust and joy in the Lord. In essence we keep God first and pray daily to grow more into the likeness of Christ. We recall Jesus' admonition as recorded in Mark 10:15: "*I tell you the truth, anyone who will not receive the kingdom of God like a little child will never enter it.*" Finally, we live the lyrics of our little worship song and do what it says: shine our light "*Everywhere we go, all around the neighborhood, all around the world,*" and we never ever "*hide it under a bushel!*"

Then our self-constructed images will fall by the wayside, and the light of Christ will fill the emptied spaces as the darkness recedes and the world will glorify not us, but the God in us as manifested by the glow of His Light.

Prayer: Thank you, Father God, for proclaiming us as Lights of the world. We know it is only by Your grace that we are. We know also that to carry that title, daily we must submit our ways to yours. Help us to do so. In Jesus' name we pray. Amen.

Reflection: What resonates most with you in either the scripture or commentary or both as it relates to your spiritual journey.

Faith Response:

HUSH!

"You have heard it was said, love your neighbor and hate your enemy., But I tell you, love your enemies and pray for those who persecute you that you may be children of your Father in heaven. He causes His sun to rise on the evil and the good and sends rain on the righteous and the unrighteous. If you love those who love you, what reward will you get? … And if you greet only your own people, what are you doing more than others? Do not even pagans do that? Be perfect therefore as your heavenly Father is perfect."
~Matthew 5:43–48

When Jesus gets to this section of His teachings, we can almost see the disciples sending furtive glances to one another. *"Love my enemy! Pray for him! Did He really say that! Surely, He doesn't expect that of us!"* We get it, don't we? Expectations such as these seem so unrealistic. They make us feel uncomfortable. We squirm in our seats even now when we hear them, as the disciples probably did seated on the rocks and ledges of that mountain site. The Bible doesn't delve into the actual initial impact these words may have had upon the forerunners of our faith. We have only their actions in the years that followed Jesus' "Principles of Discipleship" (my term) sermon to provide that insight. And from what has evolved in our understanding is that Jesus meant every word He said, and the disciples taught just that in spreading His teachings throughout the known world.

Fast forward to Ano Domino 2025. I think it's safe to say that we of the Christian faith struggle as much as those who are not with this teaching of Christ. And because we do, we've become masters of a defensive posture that employs counter arguments. We've tweaked who we perceive as our neighbor and our enemy. We've massaged the meaning of love. We pray rote prayers filled with lots of words but having little substance. We rationalize our actions despite their lack of resemblance to what Jesus spoke. Our hearts remain as shut as our windows on wintry nights against anyone who causes us grief, who doesn't fit within our social or economic circles or spheres, who are different from us in appearance, in faith, in ethnicity, in race, in gender. And perhaps the saddest result of our efforts to conform to the teaching is that all of humanity suffers the consequences of our failure to love as Jesus told and tells us to.

Maybe our failure is in the dimensions of the word's concepts. After all, love is both a noun and a verb. It is something felt and perceived. It is something demonstrated in behavior and actions. Jesus' words affirm those of the wisdom writer in Proverbs 25:21: *"If your enemy is hungry, give him something to eat; if he is thirsty, give him water to drink."* Both declarations demonstrate love in action. During His three years ministry, He modeled what He spoke. He refused to hate those who were hateful, who persecuted and railed against His teachings. Instead, He targeted them, declaring at one point that He had not come to call those who were righteous, but those who were sinners; (Matthew 9:13) in other words, the very ones who were His enemies. In the brief time of His presence on earth, we see what loving those who fall under the category of our enemy or adversary, rather than neighbor or more accurately "friend," must look like. Irrespective of how they make us feel, or how disgusted we are by their behaviors, Jesus tells us to love them, to pray for them, to be cordial to them; and to realize that God's grace falls upon us all.

Oh, I know it's a hard concept to process. The folks we've placed in our mental "enemy camp" can so easily drive us to un-Christlike attitudes and reactions. But as disciples of Jesus, we are called to perfection, as He is perfect. It's an ongoing process; we're on His potter's wheel until the moment of our final spin. Hopefully, by then we will be vessels in which love is clearly marked by our actions; and can exclaim with the psalmist, "*The Lord is with me; he is my helper. I will look with triumph on my enemies.*" (Psalm 118:7)

Prayer: Father God, we confess these words you taught are difficult to digest, especially now. The enemies we face come from all directions and in a myriad of dimensions. Daily, we ask for wisdom in our responses. Keep us mindful that all sin and come short of your glory. That includes us. As we accept your grace and forgiveness, help us to extend the same to others, most surely our enemies. In Jesus' name. Amen.

Reflection: What resonates most with you in either the scripture or commentary or both as it relates to your own spiritual journey.

FaithResponse:

HUSH!

"Therefore, do not worry about tomorrow, for tomorrow will worry about itself. Each day has enough trouble of its own."
~Matthew 6:34

Jesus had covered quite a range of topics by the close of chapter six in Matthew's Gospel. His lesson plan for His followers included the dos and don'ts of praying; including instructing them to avoid excess babbling like pagans or positioning themselves to be seen by others as they prayed; the reasons for not storing up earthly treasures; the impossibility of serving both God and money and other standards they were to practice. The verse above concludes the chapter. It's a familiar one. Preceding it, Jesus offered examples (as any teacher worth his/her salt does) why worrying was an unnecessary and fruitless emotional response to life's challenges:

- birds living out their purposes without apparent anxiety because God provides their provisions
- flowers growing in and out of season without labor or spin, adorned in a splendor that exceeds any man can produce.

Surely, Jesus implied, if these simple things of nature thrive in their appointed time and space worry-free because of God's provision, humans who were created in God's own image and have more value as a result should know He will meet their various and sundry needs. So, "the elephant in the room," for we 21st century believers is the question, "Why is worrying still such a common a response to life's challenges?" Verse 27 is emphatic: *"Can any one of you by worrying add a single hour to your life?"* The obvious answer to it then as now is "No." That admission of our powerlessness stings; but is necessary. If worrying gains us nothing, why do we still give it room in our faith toolbox, taking up space that should be filled by other more useful faith skillsets.

Does the answer perhaps rest in that hardest of postures for us to assume: surrender of our will to God's? Oh, we mouth that we do. We sing, "*I surrender all. All to thee my blessed Savior, I surrender all.*" And then the curveball comes crashing through the window: the test results, despite the earnest petitions of our prayer warriors, are devastating; the loved one with addictions relapses and ends up on our doorstep; depression stalks a young person in our life; the grim reaper appears out of nowhere and we wander in Grief City seeking our way back to wholeness and peace. Worry prepares to take the stage. And if we still struggle with the concept of who our Boss is, then it will assume a starring role.

Defeating and denying worry any time in the spotlight of your life is a goal that must be pursued daily. It requires a true confession from you that you do still attempt to "fix" stuff; to figure out what needs to be done and do it your way. You pray to God to rubber stamp your efforts or you pray about them after you're put them into play. Sorry, dear fellow pilgrim, in the vernacular of the street, "*It don't work that way.*" I offer the following "Ban Worry" strategies:

- memorize some little catch phrases sprinkled with scriptures you repeat aloud the moment Worry lands on your shoulder
- set up a playlist of your favorite anti-worry gospels songs—put on your headphones and allow them to drown out Worry's siren song
- Call your BFF or SBAM or Prayer Partner and pray in the moment until Worry realizes its power is not working today
- Stop and pray in the moment and don't quit until you know you've burst Worry's bubble once again

Some of these suggestions may sound quirky. That's okay. Come up with your own. Just begin by owning that you are not the boss; God is in control; worrying about anything does not bring about change. It's a waste of your time; and since you don't know how much of that commodity—time—you have, why give any of it over to worrying. Listen to the world's greatest teacher: DO NOT WORRY.

Prayer: Father God, we so need you to help us with this default behavior that we know is against your teaching. Strengthen us daily to mature in this area of our faith so that sooner than later, worrying disappears from our toolbox of faith. In Jesus' name. Amen.

Reflection: What resonates most with you in either the scripture or commentary or both as it relates to your spiritual journey.

Faith Response:

HUSH!

"Come to me, all of you who are weary and burdened, and I will give you rest. Take my yoke upon you and learn from me, for I am gentle and humble in heart, and you will find rest for your souls. For my yoke is easy and my burden is light."

~Matthew 11:28–30

At the time of this proclamation, Jesus had completed His introductory discipleship course for the twelve disciples and begun His ministry throughout the towns of Galilee. His words were directed at the crowds that gathered around Him. Most of them lived in rural areas, engaged in occupations common to an agrarian society. Under Roman rule, they were subject to the distinctions of class; the majority who followed Him comprising the lower level of social rankings. When Jesus used the term "yoke," they would have understood His metaphor. Their livelihood depended upon the use of yokes (wooden crossbars) which enabled their ox or oxen to pull the plows or carts of their trade. They understood the burden the animals endured when under the yoke was like the burdens they carried: oppression and persecution, third-class citizenship, physical and spiritual poverty. His words offered not further heaviness, but deliverance, rest, and hope for something better. That offer of deliverance was simple: "Come to me. Find rest for your souls. My yoke is easy. My burden is light."

Little has changed in the eons that separate us from that moment in our biblical history when Jesus held the mic, and the crowd feasted upon His words. In this time and these places where we live and have our being, many continue to carry yokes that rest heavily and prevent them from knowing God and the promises of the words He spoke that day. For reasons hard to fathom, many continue to seek relief and rest from sources that are temporary and fleeting. New age philosophies abound. Pagan-like practices parade their solutions. Offers by self-ordained gurus and experts promise to solve your problems with just a three-month free introductory fee and a year's contract.

At some point, with prayer and a willingness to accept God at His word, we who know Him because we've accepted Him and those who are still in search of Him are well advised to stop, to be still and just "Hush." His words are eternal. He has created us with physical and spiritual ears to hear them. We know Him as the God who does not lie; the God who longs to shelter us in the shadow of His wings; the God whose words have more value than gold or crypto coins. His words and the promises therein free us from worry. They reassure us of His love, healing, comfort and peace. When we come at His invitation to Him, surrendering our will to His, the yokes we carry, whether self-imposed or placed upon us by situations or challenges over which we little control, we grow in relationship with our Father God. And it is within that relationship that we are positioned to receive the promises of His words—His gentleness, compassion, ease, lightness even as we bear the burdens of our humanity.

Prayer: Father God, your words are spoken with such clarity. Open our hearts, minds and ears to hear you as if we are standing along with those to whom you spoke long ago. Your message is a tonic for the weariness we carry. May we oversaturate ourselves with it and thus turn our weariness into invigorated worship and kingdom service. Amen.

Reflection: What are the sources of your weariness and burdens? Do the chapter scriptures provide release or point you in a direction that may? Share your thoughts and take-aways below.

Faith Response:

HUSH!

When Jesus saw this, he was indignant. He said to them, "Let the little children come to me, and do not hinder them, for the kingdom of God belongs to such as these. I tell you the truth, anyone who will not receive the kingdom of God like a little child will never enter it."
~Mark 10: 14–15

Jesus was in the city of Capernaum near the Sea of Galilee when the incident regarding children occurred. In those days, babysitters, nannies, and daycare centers were absent from the scene and the little ones accompanied whoever were their guardians or care givers. As they listened and watched this man of miracles, it's understandable they would want the children to be touched and blessed by Him. Such behavior however was not looked upon favorably. It was perhaps the nascent stage of the *"children should be seen and not heard"* ideology. At any rate, Jesus' disciples responded to this invasion of His personal space by preventing the children from being placed within His reach. The scene that played out before Jesus addressed the situation might be one to which we can relate, either by being so treated during our childhood, or being of the mindset that it's an appropriate one for children. Jesus however continued His shattering of societal norms by rebuking the actions of His disciples. *"Let them come, do not hinder them,"* He spoke for all to hear. And as if to add injury to insult, He concluded with verse fifteen that in modern speak means, *"you can forget about getting into Heaven if you've lost the essence of childhood."*

What, we ask, does He mean? What do children have that gives them a ticket to Heaven, so to speak? What is it about them that's different than adults and apparently guarantees their entrance? The renown author C.S. Lewis wrote *"God wants a child's heart and a grownup head."* (Children, Heart, Want) That's a rather succinct characterization of children. They have hearts that are trusting and compassionate, kind and loving, and of course dependent. If you are a parent, grandparent, aunt, uncle, teacher, pastor, coach, you know too they are primarily literal beings; nuances often escape them. They are joyful, playful and are amazingly sincere. An anonymous writer said of them, *"Children are great imitators. So give them something to imitate."* I think that's what Jesus was seeking to help His disciples understand. Despite His words to them in Matthew 18:1–3, *"At that time the disciples came to Jesus and asked, 'Who then is the greatest in the kingdom of heaven?' He called a little child to him, and said: 'Truly I tell you, unless you change and become like little children, you will never enter the kingdom of heaven,'"* they still didn't get it. Their efforts to bar the children's access to the Savior underscore that. Perhaps the source of their confusion rests in not understanding there is a difference between being "childlike" and "childish." Typically, childish behavior is behavior unbecoming of one's age, whereas childlike behavior connotes more positive qualities such as innocence and trust. With this understanding of the semantics of the two words, we conclude Jesus meant adults ought not imitate the self-centeredness or immaturity of children but rather their innocence, their wonder, and trust in those upon whom they depended.

The message for us is a simple one. Believers who expect to be among the crowd that *"enters the kingdom of heaven"* are those whose lives emulate children in their relationship with God and neighbor. They are the kindness distributors, the doers of love actions, the models of unpretentiousness, the givers of compassion whenever it's needful, the joy givers who spread it everywhere they go, the curious who seek to know the Lord more and to share that knowledge with others, the models for what it means to trust God no matter what challenges confront them, and to depend upon Him for their needs. Finally, those who expect their ticket through the Pearly Gates to be unchallenged are the ones who have imitated Christ along their journey. What better worship of Him than to have lived a life of imitating Him in spirit, in actions and in truth, like a little child.

Prayer: Father God, we confess too often we ignore these words You spoke regarding the attributes expected of us who call you Lord. If anything, we score more highly in the column headed "Childish" than the one labeled "Childlike." Forgive us and help us daily to make the distinction between them.

Reflection: Is it possible to be childlike and grown-up at the same time? What spoke to you most in this day's lesson?

Faith Response:

HUSH!

"Do not judge, and you will not be judged. Do not condemn and you will not be condemned. Forgive and you will be forgiven. Give, and it will be given to you. … For with the measure you use, it will be measured to you."

~Luke 6:37–38

In today's lesson, Jesus follows up His teachings about loving enemies with these words as penned by the Apostle Luke. The Savior instructed them and the accompanying crowd of followers with forthrightness. Such candor was second nature to Him. Endowed with truth, He wasn't someone who sugarcoated His message; if there was a sting to it, only those who were doers of the opposite would feel it. With little doubt, He knew many would disagree with this command. Leading that group would be the religious and secular leaders of the day; and following close behind the Jane and John Does of the time who were quick to point to the "speck" in someone else's eye.

Fast-forwarding to our space and time, we read the message He uttered and more likely than not, cringe as did those who heard Him then. For if we are truthful, we own our propensity to "judge first and ask questions later." Think for a few minutes about what goes through your mind when you observe, read or hear about any of the following:

- The disreputable looking man or woman holding a sign at an intersection that reads, "hungry, please help."
- The tattooed, blue and green spiked hair, swollen belly teenage girl walking into a store.

- The frazzled mother of multiple children hanging onto the grocery store cart as she holds up the line searching for funds in her purse to pay for the sugared cereals, soda and packaged food items at the cash register.
- The student who roams a school campus with a weapon he uses to take the lives of children and staff members.
- The respected pastor who is arrested for behavior that betrays the faith he represents.
- The children whose needs are beyond the abilities of those charged with meeting them.
- The immigrant who speaks no English.
- The elected officials whose policies are abhorrent to you.

I think you understand my point. In these instances that dot the landscape of our century, where you find yourself seeing what another is doing or has done and making the judgment it's wrong; when you don't have the facts, just rumors and innuendos or social media input, you are judging. You are condemning others for what you perceive they have done or failed to do. Even in the cases where you might be right, still you are wrong because Jesus said we are not to judge or condemn. He desires us to be compassionate rather than critical, knowing that is exactly what we would hope to receive if the proverbial "shoe was on the other foot."

I accept that for many this theme is difficult to digest. So many offenses of man's inhumanity to man today violate our perceptions of what is right as the opposite seems to hold sway. Despite this reality, Jesus' words force us to delve deeper into our profession of faith. In an era that demands judgment to obtain justice which we feel we are due, what are we to do? Is it an impossibility for our time and experiences? In all transparency, I admit this command is a hard one to obey. Doing so requires constant attention to our feelings, our thoughts, our actions or lack thereof. Maybe it helps to know that according to Open Bible Info, 100 Bible verses reference judging others. The more notable ones being, in addition to the day's verse, Matthew 7:1–5, John 8:1–8, James 4:11–12, Romans 2:1–3, Romans 12:16–18, and 2 Corinthians 5:10. As challenging as these words Jesus spoke are to live by, the only alternative to obeying them is not to. For the beloved community, that is not possible. So, in the vernacular of the idiom, we *"put on our big girl/boy panties/pants,"* (i.e. choose responses and behaviors that demonstrate our maturity in faith and obedience to God's word) and daily strive to use whatever mnemonic devices we can to help us to reject judging others. Memorizing verses to repeat to yourself at "judgmental moments" may be a good start.

Prayer: Father God, thank you for being our strong tower when the enemy of our faith tries to lead us astray, for that is exactly what the nuances of the life journey present daily. Give us discernment and courage to confront the temptation of judging in the very instance it presents itself. Speak to us in that moment a verse that redirects our thinking and helps us back upon the path to eternity. In Jesus' name we pray.

Reflection: Is there conviction or confirmation for you in today's lesson? Explain in the faith response section below.

Faith Response:

HUSH!

Jesus said to his disciples, "Therefore I tell you. do not worry about your life, what you will eat, or about your body, what you will wear. For life is more than food, and the body more than clothing. … And can any of you by worrying add a single hour to your span of life?"
~Luke 12:22–23;25 NRSV

A recent newspaper headline read that the state of Texas led the nation in "food insecurity," affecting one in every five children in North Texas. Such declarations of food shortages have become so common, not just in Texas but around the country, that the shocking effect of this food crisis in a nation of such wealth is minimal. In large cities, small towns or rural counties, food, specifically the lack thereof, is a grim reality for many. Food pantry ministries in churches, food banks operated by non-profit organizations, and individual efforts to "feed the homeless and hungry" on city streets have become a mainstay of the modern landscape. Coupled with the food issues obviously are the cousins "clothing" and "housing," Together the triad continues to haunt us as social dilemmas needing resolution.

With this contemporary backdrop, our chapter verses may give pause. While His statement that we're incapable of adding an hour to our life span is one most will say, "Amen" to, the words referencing sustenance and shelter are a little more difficult to sort out. Literally, they suggest that the lack of food or clothing are issues believers should not be concerned about or rather worry about. Yet, we know that is not the case. Both believers and non-believers, for a variety of reasons, deal with these shortages every day and they do worry.

What then are we to conclude about these words of Jesus in relationship to the truth of our times? Are we as modern-day disciples to simply say to those caught in webs of worry because they lack these necessities of life, *"Don't worry. God knows what you need."* I don't think so.

Both the Old and New Testaments provide guidance. They clarify for us our role within the beloved community of faith that lends relevance to it today. And though as His disciples we know that "worrying" is an unproductive exercise and have learned faith strategies to keep it at bay, many of our fellow travelers have not. As we are the *"body of Christ and individual members of it,"* (1 Corinthians 12:27 ESV), we are charged to care for those who rightfully worry when they are without the resources to sustain themselves. Oh, we may offer encouragement by voicing the words, *"Don't worry, God knows."* But our faith witness demands more:

- *"He who oppresses the poor shows contempt for their Maker, but whoever is kind to the needy honors God."* Proverbs 14:31
- *"He who is kind to the poor lends to the Lord, and he will reward him for what he has done."* Proverbs 19:17
- *"Anyone who has two shirts should share with the one who has none, and anyone who has food should do the same."* Luke 3:11
- *"Lord, when did we see you hungry and feed you, or thirsty and give you something to drink? …Or needing clothes and clothe you? … The King will reply, 'Truly I tell you, whatever you did for one of the least of these brothers and sisters of mine, you did it for me.'"* Matthew 25:37–40

Worrying is futile, a waste of brain power and a stealer of peace. Jesus knew that just as He knew that in our humanness, we are prone to it. But He also knew that those who would be disciples must be its fiercest resisters. Our best weapons are giving life to the words in His Word: *"to loose the chains of injustice and untie the cords of the yoke, to set the oppressed free and break every yoke … to share your food with the hungry and to provide the wanderer with shelter—when you see the naked, to clothe them …"* Isaiah 6–7 It is in the exercise of our faith that worrying loses its power and the command of Jesus becomes a natural state. And who knows? Perhaps in living out our faith, we will bring hope to those in need. Their sense of hopelessness may diminish as their needs for food, clothing and shelter are met, and their worrying about the things Jesus says not to worry about will follow suit.

Prayer: Father God, You know that despite your command to not worry that we do. As often as we say we'll stop, somehow worrying is our default position. Even if we pray about it, worrying lingers long after our "Amen." Help us to deepen our understanding of the peace we forfeit because we can't give it up. Make us non-worriers by addressing the needs of those who have concrete reasons for concern regarding life's necessities. In Jesus' name. Amen.

Reflection: Be honest. What did this lesson suggest of where you stand today on your faith journey as it relates to being a worrier? What strategies can you commit to lessen worry's hold?

Faith Response:

HUSH!

"Martha, Martha," the Lord answered, "you are worried and upset about many things, but only one thing is needed. Mary has chosen what is better, and it will not be taken away from her."
~Luke 10:41–42

few years ago, I bought a tee shirt imprinted with the words: *"Be a Mary in a Martha World."* In these senior years, I've enjoyed wearing novelty tees bearing biblical or bookish messages. This one had a new home. The lesson scripture is a familiar one and probably resonates more with women than men. We imagine Jesus in a relaxed mood, as He sat on the floor mats that were the sofas of His time, continuing to teach as dinner preparations were underway. The two sisters, Mary and Martha, shared the home, but for some reason, only one was laboring away in preparation for the meal. The scene of the scripture unfolds during a time when women were the household executors, responsible for all hosting duties. Upon their shoulders rested any and everything attendant to hospitality. The disciples and other men would be the ones surrounding Jesus at such times as this one. Yet, there Mary sat among the host of men giving rapt attention to Jesus' words.

Continuing in our imagination of the moment, we can picture the dutiful Martha beginning to wonder where Mary was. Why was she lingering in the other room with all the two of them needed to do? Finally, in exasperation, she goes in and espies Mary calmly listening as Jesus spoke. Oh, the thoughts that must have bounced around in her head at that moment. We won't speculate. We simply applaud her rather respectful query: "*Lord, don't you care that my sister has left me to do the work by myself? Tell her to help me!*" (Luke 10:40) As the chapter verse so reads, Jesus responded.

Fast forward two thousand plus years. If the truth is told, many of us, as we say in the vernacular of our times, "feel you," Martha. In other words, we understand her frustration. Stuff must get done; somebody must do the work, attend to the details, right? In His mild rebuke of the industrious Martha, what point is Jesus making? What does He want her and us to understand? Did a contemplative spirit trump an industrious one in that situation?

Perhaps we understand the answer to the question within the concepts of time and place. "*There is a time for everything, and a season for every activity under heaven…*"These iconic words of Ecclesiastes 3:1 help clarify this encounter of the sisters with Jesus. In a scene that began with a spirit of hospitality as modeled by Martha with her invitation to Jesus and the disciples, two forces met head-to-head: time and season. The stay at the sisters' home was temporary. In a sense, Jesus was "on the clock." His ministry in this first coming had a predetermined ending date. For whatever reason, one sister decided the visit was a time to offer hospitality (which automatically meant preparation and work) and the other sister chose the visit as a time for listening and learning from the Teacher. His response to Martha suggests the season of that moment was better understood by Mary. Yes, hospitality was important and had its place; but more important than hospitality was the reason He was even there—to teach and preach the gospel of good news to all who would hear Him. Mary got it and made a conscious decision to throw her apron aside and find an inconspicuous place to listen to Jesus. A clean house and abundant table could not provide that; only seeking His face and being in His presence hearing Him speak would. Martha forfeited that experience with her preoccupation with secular pursuits. Mary chose the sacredness of moments with the impending Savior. There is a time for industriousness and there is a time for pensiveness.

What then do we glean from this story? As it was for the two sisters, it is for us. God expects us to do the work He's appointed us to do, but not at the exclusion of quiet and reflective time with

Him, hearing Him as He "speaks" through the medium of our time to better ascertain His purposes and plans.

Prayer: Father God, help us. We live in a "Martha" world where we are measured and judged by what we do and how we do it. The frenzy of our "doing" matches that of deep-sea mammals circling a prey. Without your divine intervention, we admit we are probably more like Martha than we are like Mary. We pray for grace to flip that tendency, sooner than later. In Jesus' name. Amen.

Reflection: Who are you more like—Martha or Mary? Does your current lifestyle demand industriousness? Within the myriad responsibilities on your plate, how likely are you to deliberately set aside significant time to "hear" the Lord speaking to you via His written word? Or do you only get some Bible/Jesus time in as your schedule so allows? Be honest in your self-examination.

Faith Response:

HUSH!

"No servant can serve two masters. Either he will hate one and love the other, or he will be devoted to one and despise the other. You cannot serve both God and money."

~Luke 16:13

At the time Jesus spoke these words, He was in the home of a prominent Pharisee who had invited him over for "discussion," not because he wanted to understand Jesus' teachings, but so he might trap Him into contradicting the Jewish law. Jesus proceeded to use the "discussion" time to teach by way of parables the Good News He had come to proclaim. The Pharisees loved money and thought one's status was determined by one's wealth. To them, this carpenter's teachings regarding its value were nonsensical. As Jesus continued speaking, He offered His listeners an alternative life-view regarding money's perceived power; it could never compete with what only God provides.

Today's scripture is timely because in many ways, we think and act like the Pharisees. We live in a time when the attempt to do just what Jesus said we cannot do is not unusual. Some of us serve not just two, but multiple masters. We are adept at balancing (to our way of thinking anyway) both the "secular" and the "sacred" to do so. Essentially, what we've done is tweak the notion that to simultaneously love or be devoted to someone or something is an impossibility as Jesus spoke it was by assigning to each its own niche in our lives. Gone is Jesus' premise and in turn from a fallacious stance, we live dishonestly.

Money or the love of it can easily take the place in one's life that should be reserved for God. The human preoccupation with it elevates its importance. The more of it we have, the more of it we desire and strive to attain. The opposite holds true—the less of it we have, the more of it we desire and strive to acquire. So, whether we have more or less of it, it has authority, sway, leverage, power, influence. Money is the commodity that drives the secular world. And therein rests Jesus' contention. It is impossible to accord God primacy at the same time we kneel at money's altar seeking the power it bestows.

"And God spoke all these words: … 'You shall have no other gods before me.'" (Exodus 20:1,3) In the home of someone who professed strict observance of traditional and written Jewish law, Jesus challenged the host with the words that echoed what God had spoken to Moses. This was not new theology, but fulfillment of the Law. To the very sect that claimed religious superiority and knowledge of the law, Jesus called them out for violating it. The allegiance to money and wealth had become their gods, and in bowing to it, they disobeyed the very law they proclaimed to uphold.

If we're honest, we'll admit that the money god is alive and kicking, continuing today to grant privilege and power to its possessors. A well-known quote attributed to the 19th century British Lord Acton sums up what the scriptural warning implies when we grant lordship to the money and power twins. *"Power tends to corrupt and absolute power corrupts absolutely."* An apt rendering of the divine words spoken in Exodus and Luke and as relevant here in the 21st century. Scripture teaches us we are to *"be in the world, but of the world."* With that as our thesis for godly living, the only gods we give allegiance to are God the Father and Jesus Christ, His Son. They are our authority. They are our power. They alone hold sway over us, not our possessions, our money or lack thereof of either. We, like Paul, are content in whatever circumstances we face. We've made the choice.

Prayer: Father God, in our strength we struggle to obey these directives You and Christ have spoken to us. Too easily we succumb to secular pursuits, desires, wants and perceived needs and by so doing find ourselves serving not You but the secular. Help us daily to yield not to those influences, but only to your word. In Jesus' name we pray. Amen.

Reflection: Are there areas of your life in which you've replaced God's authority and power with the secular gods of money and power or influence? Reflect upon the lesson within that context. Record your reflections below.

Faith Response:

HUSH!

Jesus said to her, "I am the resurrection and the life. He who believes in me will live, even though he dies; and whoever lives and believes in me will never die. Do you believe this?"

~John 11:25–26

In the eleventh chapter of John's Gospel, the apostle records our Savior in a memorable moment when both His humanness and divinity are on display. Sisters of His friend Lazarus get word to Him to come because Lasarus is ill. Knowing of Jesus' powers, they trust that He will arrive in time to heal their brother. As scripture reads, Jesus deliberately delayed the return to Lazarus' home and by the time He did arrive, Lazarus was dead; and not just dead but buried. Of course, the sisters were both bereft and bewildered. *"Lord, if you had been here, my brother would not have died."* Contemporary translation: *"What took you so long? You could have saved him if You had come when we sent the message!"* As the sisters dissolved in tears and friends gathered there with them followed suit, Jesus was moved and troubled to the point that as scripture reads, *"Jesus wept."* Now the Bible doesn't tell us if at that point, someone handed the Savior a cloth to wipe away His tears or He used the sleeve of His robe, but soon after the display of human emotions, Jesus approached the tomb where His friend lay in grave clothes. And there, after lifting His eyes to heaven and praying, Jesus shouted, *"Lazarus, come out!"* And the friend who was dead walked out of the tomb alive.

Talk about a moment to just HUSH! Surely, this one qualifies. The Jesus of the preceding account is the same Jesus we profess to believe in today, some two thousand plus year later. The words of comfort He spoke to Mary and Martha are unchanged. He speaks to us the same. The question He posed lingers. "*Do you believe this?*" To say "yes" to that question is to live your faith in a manner that demonstrates that you do. You can't just proclaim it; your thoughts and your deeds must match your utterances. If Jesus is the resurrection and the life and you profess that belief, what confirms it in the life you display to the world? Mary and Martha "kinda sorta" got it. But even they struggled. They wanted the desires of their hearts in that moment of challenge. Jesus wanted them and the community to understand who he was at a much deeper level. It was within His power to heal Lazarus from a distance. He could have arrived before the death. He chose neither of these manifestations. His purpose in that moment was to cement His identity; to open their minds and hearts to the realization that belief in and obedience to Him was a guarantee to them of eternity. As I've oft repeated, nothing has changed from God's perspective. He continues to bring the "dead" in us to life if we surrender to His will. He pursues, chasing us in the hope that eventually we'll exhaust ourselves in life outside His design. He waits for our surrender, so that the life we live can answer for us, "Yes, I believe." God is the CEO of the Comfort and Resurrection Business. Stop hindering His efforts to bring you on board.

Prayer: Father God, oh that today might be the day I fully and finally surrender all to you. The day when my faith profession matches my faith walk. You are my resurrection and my life. Forgive me for refusing to live as if that is my belief. In Jesus' name. Amen.

Reflection: What are your thoughts? Did the lessen enlighten or confirm your faith witness? Reflect and respond below.

Faith Response:

HUSH!

"Do not let your hearts be troubled. Trust in God; trust also in me."
~John 14:1

It was at the observance of the Passover Feast that Jesus said today's chapter verse to the twelve disciples. What was traditionally a time of celebration had turned somber as Jesus spoke of disturbing imminent events. One of the disciples would betray Him He said, and Peter (upon whom Jesus had declared the church would be established), would deny Him. Thus, they were not a joyful bunch as their time together continued. Ever sensitive to the fact that their decision to follow Him would be challenging and demoralizing when His mission was completed and He returned to God, the Father, Jesus began offering words of comfort. The three verses that follow the one above give the disciples reasons not to despair. He would prepare homes for them in the place He was returning to, and there would be sufficient room for all. Additionally, not only would He prepare for their eventual reunion, but He also promised to come back to get them.

These words of comfort Jesus spoke then He speaks today. Each time we read them or hear them read to us, the message is unchanged. Broken into declarations, it commands us to: refuse to be troubled, trust God and trust Jesus. Nowhere within the scripture is a suggestion that "trouble" would not dog us. Quite the opposite, at that very moment they were a down-hearted, depressed, worried, anxious group. A sense of trouble held sway. It's easy to understand their emotional state. We experience it ourselves when life comes apart at the seams. Questions with no answers tumble about in our minds. Yet, the Savior said and says, "Do not be troubled."

We know what they were thinking when He spoke because we think the same: "*How can I not be?*" I suggest the following: Open your "Handbook of Comfort" and ingest some of the ingredients it offers as remedies:

- Lean not on your own understanding and God will direct your path (Proverbs 3:5–6)
- Seek God for He does not forsake those who do. (Psalm 9:10)
- Be strong and courageous during difficult seasons for God is with you wherever you go. (Joshua 1:9)
- God's word declares that He has plans to give you a future and a hope. (Jeremiah 29:11)
- Do not be afraid for God is your salvation, your strength and defense. (Isaiah 12:2)
- *"Blessed be the God and Father of our Lord Jesus Christ, the Father of mercies and God of all comfort, who comforts us in all our trib-ulations."* (2 Corinthians 1:3 NKJV)

Believers who strive for maturity in faith take to heart the Lord's spoken words, from both the Old and New Testaments. They have learned that saturation in them on a consistent basis is a surefire method of dissuading trouble from thinking it can have a seat at your table whenever it wants to.

Prayer: Father God, as much as we say we believe, we know that sometimes that belief is tested and we waver. Confusion creeps in and before we can put a cap on it, Trouble's on-stage throwing darts at our faith. Help us to recall in such moments that we have already what is needed to turn the tide and bring down the curtains on this downer of peace. In Jesus' name, we pray. Amen.

Reflection: Are you easily troubled in spirit when challenges or trials take center stage in your life? Does the lesson scripture help? Share your thoughts in the space provided.

Faith Response:

JUNETEENTH

"I am the Lord your God, who brought you out of Egypt to be your God. I am the Lord your God."

~Numbers 15:41

"Fix these words of mine in your hearts and mind…"

~Deuteronomy 11:18

Today, the nation celebrates a novice national holiday commonly known as "Juneteenth." Signed into law just four years ago, it commemorates the emancipation of enslaved people in this country. The original date of the act that "freed" those who were considered property rather than people was January 1, 1863. However, the news didn't reach the new citizens in the state of Texas until June 19, 1865. And viola! Juneteenth was born and thereafter celebrated within the African American community each year. In fact, the 19th of June celebration held as much significance for the formerly enslaved and their subsequent descendants as did the 4th of July. If not, more so.

Some three thousand plus years ago, God declared who He was to the Israelites whom He'd freed from bondage in Egypt. As they built new lives as a freed people, God reminded them of the role He had played. He delivered them to be their God. And as time passed, He told them to "fix" or write His words in their hearts and minds so that they might not sin against Him, their Deliverer.

In this time and space of the 21st century, we who as it has been written were *"kissed by the sun"* and others who struggle beneath the yokes of oppression, discrimination, inequality, poverty, exclusion best understand the significance of today. It is not just a recognition of a wrong eventually corrected, at least on paper, it is more urgently a call to action. Dual action. God's words if indeed we have written them on our hearts and carry them in our minds as He has commanded require two things. Not discounting the parades and other festivities that mark the holiday, we as God's beloved community are called to a reexamination of our hearts and minds in the realities of our time. Are we truly invested in living as God and Jesus commanded? Does our lifestyle reflect obedience to their words? Once the balloons have floated away, the bands have disbursed, the barbeque fixings have been consumed, and the last dance of the night has ended, will God see in the descendants of those whom He delivered three thousand years ago and the descendants of those set free one hundred sixty-two years ago spirits of obedience and unceasing efforts to live as He commanded? If your answer gives pause, perhaps it's because of the realization that though we know what the Lord requires of us, follow through is inconsistent at best. Our biblical ancestors had a plethora of laws to which they were to adhere. Jesus simplified it when He said, *"Love the Lord your God with all your heart and with all soul and with all your mind. This is the first and greatest commandment. And the second is like it: 'Love your neighbor as yourself.' All the Law and the Prophets hang on these two commandments."* Matthew 22:36–40

As we commemorate another Juneteenth with the world in disarray, may we find the courage to live as the delivered people of God who are committed to obedience to His words.

HUSH!

"If you love me, you will obey what I command."

~John 14:15

Jesus spoke the chapter verse while He and the disciples continued in observance of the Passover. His earlier words of comfort were not intended to overshadow the essence of His message, and they needed to understand that. *"Obedience is better than sacrifice…"* (1Samuel 15:22) was a command they would have been exposed to. Jesus' use of a "conditional sentence" to express it might have been warranted by the shakiness of their faith at that moment, as well as fear of what was to come. Conditional sentences pose hypothetical conditions and their possible outcomes. *"If you love me"* is Jesus' hypothesis and the possible outcome of the hypothesis is *"you will obey what I command."* In those moments leading to the eventual crucifixion, the disciples were understandably not just fearful, but anxious and probably confused. By all accounts these were simple men, not a Torah advanced placement scholar among them. So, Jesus kept it simple: Love me? Do what I told you to do.

In the brief years before this encounter, Jesus had done a ton of teaching. And because it was primarily an oral culture—writing among the common man being unlikely—the disciples' memories had to serve as the repository for what the Lord commanded. Loving Him was a no-brainer. They'd demonstrated their love, their allegiance by leaving all to follow Him. But obedience was tricky. To obey meant to remember the teachings. Could they? Would they? God had a Plan B already in play. Neither He nor

His Son were taking any chances. Jesus followed the chapter verse with: "*I will ask the Father and He will give you another Counselor to be with you forever—the Spirit of truth.*" (John 14:16) We might think of the Counselor, i.e. the Holy Spirit as their spiritual "cheat sheet." If at anytime they forgot what Jesus had commanded, they could go to the Counselor who had the right answers and right directions to get back on course. Additionally, the Holy Spirit would inspire and inform the later apostles whom God would call to spread the gospel message the original disciples preached.

Because God's word is timeless and eternal, we who follow Him today need not cringe at the words Jesus spoke to His first followers and think they are impossible for us in the fallen world in which we live. God's Plan B for us is not complicated. The Bible teaches and gives guidance, so we can obey what Jesus commands.

> "*We know that we have come to know him if we obey his commands. The man who says. 'I know him' but does not do what he commands is a liar, and the truth is not in him. Whoever claims to live in him must walk as Jesus did.*"
>
> ~1 John 2:3–6

Think of it perhaps as our "cheat sheet." And, in those situations, in which we are confused or tempted, the Holy Spirit, our "Spirit Whisperer," moves us toward the truth of "what thus says the Lord". It helps us avoid sin and demonstrate our love for the Savior. I think the bases are covered. If we profess to love Him, we will obey Him. Will we falter? Yes. Can we recover and gain our balance? Yes, the Bible is our resource for that. Will we sometimes be confused even after we've read the Holy Word? Yes. What will help then? The Holy Spirit is ever present. It will step in and clear confusion.

Prayer: Father God, Jesus' words are often so direct and clear. Yet, we stumble in obeying them anyway. Rid us of all that blocks our disobedience. We pray in Jesus' name. Amen.

Reflection: Does the lesson resonate with you? Is it a conformation of your faith journey or an indictment of it? Respond below.

Faith Response:

HUSH!

"I have told you these things, so that in me you may have peace. In this world you will have trouble. But take heart! I have overcome the world."

~John 16:33

At this juncture on the night of the Last Supper, Jesus spoke without parables about who He was, His mission and immediate future. Much of what they'd heard during that evening was no doubt difficult for them to "digest." We might consider the chapter verses words of encouragement and a balm for the pain they had yet to experience. Yes, Jesus was God incarnate, and all power rested within Him. If He had so chosen, He could have overthrown the tyranny of the times; but as we know that was not His mission. In the ensuing days, the disciples would witness firsthand what He meant by the words, "have overcome" the world. His imminent crucifixion, death and resurrection would solidify their meaning. In the quiet hush of that moment, Jesus spoke words for those who had answered His call and except for Judas Iscariot, followed Him. During the sorrow that would cloud their vision for a while, the words would become a stronghold.

These two thousand plus years later, the words toll still for all who have ears to hear and a heart to embrace their meaning. Today marks the mid-point of July 2025. The title of Mahalia Jackson's familiar gospel song, *"Troubles of the World,"* might easily be the catchphrase of the times. Besieged on multiple fronts by natural and man-caused disasters, wars and rumors of war, abuse of power and authority; and with integrity, morality, truthfulness, justice, compassion, mercy and kindness inching their way toward the scaffold of obliteration, in its myriad disguises trouble is firmly rooted.

As Jesus eyed their fearful expressions and uncertainties, He urged them to "take heart." In essence He wanted them to grasp the significance of what was about to happen to Him and how within that seeming tragedy, victory would emerge embedded with peace that He alone would give. Would the world's troubles disappear? No, they would not. We are living witnesses to that. Trouble snaps at our heels, hounds our steps, wreaks havoc in our homes and neighborhoods, delivers dire diagnoses in the doctor's office, and seems to control everything around us. But the encouragement of His words in that upper room is unchanged. His peace is available 24/7. In the darkness of the night, in the brightness of the day, His victory over trouble is steadfast; and because He lives, peace is ours to claim. And even though we can't always control some of the trouble that brazenly knocks on the door, and we have no recourse as it struts in, we do have a weapon to combat it during its stay. From the cross Jesus set Peace free. And what our Savior gives us, nothing can steal. Jesus Peace. It's been around a long time. It's here if we want it until eternity. Place an order if you don't have it; and watch trouble lose its sting.

Prayer: Father God, we understand that trouble was and is a definer of the fallen world in which we reside. We know that Jesus told us to "Take heart". We struggle to do that when trouble shows up. Help us to live more faithfully so that peace becomes a natural attribute of who we are especially during troubling times. In Jesus' name we pray. Amen.

Reflection: How do you react in troubling moments or situations? Is your spirit peaceful or in turmoil? How might you grow stronger in acquiring a peaceful spirit to combat trouble's influence? Respond below.

Faith Response:

HUSH!

Then Jesus said to his disciples, "Whoever wants to be my disciple must deny themselves and take up their cross and follow me. … What good will it be for someone to gain the whole world, yet forfeit their soul? Or what can anyone give in exchange for their soul?"
~Matthew 16:24, 26–27

Jesus' comments to this group of men who were already considered His disciples because they were following Him, might at first reading seem odd. They'd demonstrated already their willingness to give up their livelihoods and join the movement He led. But at this point the reality of what lay ahead for Him and them obviously had not crystallized. Jesus knew it was necessary for Him to be as clear as possible about what this meant for them and for those who were to come as the ministry spread. The Good News He preached demanded a level of commitment beyond the norm of the time. His stated requirement of denial of self and taking up their crosses was probably no more popular in the first century than now in the twenty-first.

From a modern perspective, radicalism then might have been easier. After all they lived rough lives in a predominantly agrarian society with none of the advantages afforded the priests, religious and secular authorities. Regardless of the differences between then and now however, the disciples of record understood that to be called followers of "The Way" meant turning away from life as they knew it before Jesus invaded their world. Choosing to follow His teachings required personal sacrifice, and material things that had once represented the "must haves" of a good life for which one strove to possess reevaluated in terms of what Jesus taught. As scripture so records, they (excepting Judas Iscariot) made the choice that would alter the lives of many in future generations. The level of commitment of which Jesus spoke was "off the chart" commitment. For them it would come to mean physical suffering, rejection by family and friends, loneliness, being met with hostility, and very likely death by the common method of that time: crucifixion on a cross that they themselves would carry to the execution site just as Jesus did. Understanding the consequences, the disciples made a choice. They followed Jesus.

Fast forwarding two thousand plus years, Jesus' words for those who profess Him are unchanged. In fact, they speak to us with as much urgency and intensity if not more. We must make a choice in an era of distinct social statuses based upon wealth and power. Contemporary Influencers "preach" lifestyles which in no way epitomize Christ's characterization of His followers. The very idea of deliberately denying oneself the best life has to offer, and intentionally taking on anything that might interfere with the pursuit of it seems ludicrous. Within this milieu, massaging the message by tweaking it so that commitment to it is not so literal is much easier. "*Taking up the cross*" simply means joining church, attending worship service on Sunday morning and placing something in the basket at Offering Time. "*Denying oneself*" is adhered to with donations of things we no longer use or need to local charities that assist the less fortunate.

But if we are to truly be followers of Jesus, we can't tweak the commitment, dress it up in contemporary wrappings, devise strategies to lessen its sacrificial nature, or re-word it to align with the lexicon and behaviors of the secular. Professors of Christ will pay a price for the commitment they embrace. For them, lifestyles will be different. Utilization of resources will be different. How their time is spent Monday through Saturday will be different. Their world view will be different. His words will alter everything. Like the disciples to whom Christ spoke that day, they too will follow Jesus.

Prayer: Heavenly Father God, following You is not for the fainthearted. It takes courage and commitment to live what we profess. We can't do it on our own. We need You. Shepherd us each day; let your rod and staff both guide and correct us. In Jesus' name we pray. Amen.

Reflection: Spend some quality time meditating upon the level of your commitment to Christ if you have surrendered your life to Him. Are you "denying yourself" and "taking up the cross" as His words declare? Are their actions you need to take to correct the course? Respond in the spaces below.

Faith Response:

HUSH!

When Jesus spoke again to the people, he said, "I am the light of the world. Whoever follows me will never walk in darkness but will have the light of life."

~John 8:12

Imagine the thoughts of the people hearing Jesus speak this characterization of Himself in first century Israel. Their primary sources of light at the time were the sun, the moon, the stars (unless they were obscured by clouds), and small oval shaped clay lamps that were not very bright, filled with olive oil. To hear Him proclaim that He was the light source of the entire world must have been both puzzling and mind blowing. And the added declaration that those who chose to follow Him would not need to procure light to banish darkness but would have the light of life through Him would probably be more startling. Reading His words today, we might think of Him as the original "King of Figurative Speech." In addition to parables, figurative language such as metaphors, similes, and symbolism filled His verbal toolbox as He attempted to explain who He was and why He came. For some who followed Him regularly, such expressions might have been less bewildering. Nonetheless, we can visualize the perplexed expressions on the faces of those hearing Him speak in the part of the temple where candles were burning.

To conceptualize His words within the context of what they understood the meaning of light to be was not easy. In all honesty, it's still sort of hazy for us today. What did He really mean by saying He's the "light" of the world, that those who follows Him will not walk in "darkness," and what is the "light of life?" How do we understand these metaphors in today's world and their application to our life?

We are spared some of the confusion our biblical ancestors felt at that time because of the witness and writings of those He sent to spread the good news. His teachings that merged with the essence of the Old Testament and its fulfillment of it through Him help us. The temple candles symbolized the light of God that had led the Israelites through the desert. Such artificial lighting was no longer needed to represent God's presence. Jesus Himself was that presence and the light that would lead and illuminate the journey of faith. We who give our allegiance to Him and seek to follow Him need not fear the natural darkness that comes with the close of each day, nor more importantly the "darkness" represented by the challenges inherent in our humanity. Seasons of illness, disaster, oppression, depression, poverty, fear, grief, etc. are all times in which shattered hope can sow seeds of darkness. But Jesus as our light overcomes them all. It is His power, protection and presence that ensures we who lay claim to Him need not fear. As He declared, we have "the light of life." That assurance is enough no matter what form darkness takes.

Prayer: Father God, thank you for Jesus' words that empower us to live in chaotic times without fear of the darkness that seems so prevalent. We trust the veracity of His words to these first hearers of it in ways perhaps they could not. History is on our side. We know our Redeemer lives and continues in the shepherding business today. In His name we pray. Amen.

Reflection: Are you sometimes confused by the symbolism with which Jesus speaks? What resources do you use to help you get to the essence of His words? Share your responses in the space below?

Faith Response:

HUSH!

*For God so loved the world that He gave His one and only Son,
that whoever believes in him shall not perish but have eternal life.*
~John 3:16

I had a tee shirt resembling an athletic shirt whose front was imprinted with the wording: *John 3:16 Any Questions.* I eventually gave it away. Prior to that, any time I wore it, often I'd get a nod or a smile from strangers who glanced at it and then at me. My assumption was that they were fellow believers who appreciated my tee shirt evangelism. Hearing a recent sermon titled *Unpacking John 3:16,* I realized that my assumptions over the years of sporting my scriptural tee shirt may have been flawed. That verse as I discovered on many search engines leads the list of most known or most popular Bible verses. It's captured on gift items, plagues, jewelry, posters, caps, and assorted other bric-a-brac. Such inclusion within our social milieu generated a question. Has the easy familiarity of a verse committed to memory by many children before they can even read, caused it to lose its biblical essence? Did this extraordinary expression of the extent of God's love for the world and how He demonstrated that love still inspire faithfulness and resoluteness in those who profess Him and Jesus Christ as His only Son? Or on the hand, had the commonness of its usage beyond religious settings dimmed its significance and relevance? And perhaps most importantly, does its familiarity not just affirm a profession of faith, but does it also draw those who know the words but not their true meaning to Christ? During the years of proudly wearing my faith tee, I never stopped to confirm that crucial component to as the Savior commanded, "draw all others unto Him."

Prayer: Father God, help us in our efforts to live our faith not to miss any opportunity to point others to You. Keep us free of worldliness that makes us forget your call to live in ways that point others to the Cross. In Jesus' name. Amen.

Reflection: What outreach disciplines do you regularly practice with the intent of sharing the gospel to those who may not know Jesus or may have fallen away from serving Him? Share in the spaces provided below.

Faith Response:

HUSH!

For God did not send His Son into the world to condemn the world, but to save the world through him.

~John 3:17

For millennia God had sought to engage His people in a covenant relationship that ultimately would result in their being reconciled to Him for eternity. The story of the Old Testament gives witness to what may be called an unsettling, unsustainable "emotional roller coaster ride." Through the eras of the patriarchs, prophets, judges and kings; exile and subjugation by pagan rulers, God's people experienced many highs and lows, twists and turns in often terrifying situations. When life was at its lowest, they cried out to Him, and for a while were faithful. Too often though when times were good, their allegiance weakened and easily they forgot "what thus saith the Lord," returning to behaviors outside His will; and predictably to their wailing and moaning for divine deliverance.

We marvel at God's restraint and attitude of never giving up on His wayward creation. The words of today's chapter follow John 3:16 and conclude the apostle's declaration regarding the depth and purposes of Jesus' first coming. As significant as the former chapter's verse was and is, today's stands as its equal, if not more so. With little hesitation, we admit that if Jesus had come to both offer salvation and condemnation, we would be a lost people. As such we are even more indebted to Him. God's gift had but one stipulation. We had/have to believe Jesus is His only Son. The stipulation implied in today's verse calls us to even greater reverence and worship. We carry daily the weight of our sins. In its endless loop of sinning and repenting, we can't seem to disembark from this sin "roller coaster" set on automatic. Because God loved us and knew us, His redemption plan included an escape hatch. Through Jesus' sacrifice on the cross, our sins would be absolved. His actions cancelled condemnation. What a God we serve!

Prayer: Father God, as scripture reads, *"How awesome is your name in all the earth!"* We love You in full recognition of how much more You have demonstrated your love for us. As our journey continues, help us daily to live in recognition and with gratitude for what You have done. In Jesus' name we pray. Amen.

Reflection: Do you truly understand what God has done for you and how much He loves you? Share your thoughts in the spaces below.

Faith Response:

HUSH!

After this Jesus went out and saw a tax collector by the name of Levi sitting at his tax booth. "Follow me," Jesus said to him, and Levi got up, left everything and followed him.

~Luke 5:27

In the verses that preceded Jesus' encounter with Levi, He had publicly healed a paralytic man. The religious leaders and teachers of the law were scandalized when Jesus proclaimed that because of the faith of the man's friends who carried his mat, his sins were forgiven. Then as if to drive home the mantle of His authority, Jesus said, "*get up, take up your mat and go home.*" The onlookers were amazed as the man stood and walked away praising God. We have no way of knowing if there was a time lapse between the miracle Jesus had performed at that moment; nothing suggests that the tax collector knew about the incident. *"After this"* is a vague segue to His interaction with Levi. As scripture reads, Jesus simply spoke the command, "*Follow me,*" and Levi left his work, his belongings and did just that.

Because we have only what is written as a guide, we can't say with surety why this tax collector responded as he did. We can speculate that he had seen Jesus around town, even heard Him teach and knew the local gossip regarding the miracles He was performing. But that's just speculation. All we know is that Jesus invited Levi to follow Him, and though at that moment, he might have refused—after all his was an important position in the financial arena of the times, he accepted the invitation. He followed the Savior.

I imagine you know where I'm going with this commentary. Jesus' invitation to Levi wasn't His first invite. He had begun His ministry as recorded in the Gospel of Matthew with *"Follow me"* to the two brothers Simon Peter and Andrew and soon thereafter to brothers James and John, fishermen by trade. He promised to make them *"fishers of men"* if they did. We know that eventually a total of twelve men left their livelihoods to follow Jesus. We know that as the ministry spread, others (both men and women) heard and accepted His invitation. Today, that invitation is a foundational aspect of the Christian faith. Though the "how" of it can vary within Protestant and Catholic denominations, its meaning is eternal. He speaks to anyone who hears and is willing to leave behind the trappings of the world for Him. In the quietest of moments and the most raucous, He waits. What better time than now to turn and follow the One who issues the life-changing invitation: *"Follow me."*

Prayer: Father God, thank you for the eternal invitation You spoke millennia ago. It rings now as it did then. May we who are following You be intentional in pointing those who are not to You, so that they might respond "Yes." In Your name we pray. Amen.

Reflection: Are you truly following Jesus? What is the evidence? What have you left behind since saying "Yes" to His words, *"Follow me"*? Respond below in the space provided.

Faith Response:

HUSH!

"The good man brings good things out of the good stored up in his heart, and the evil man brings evil things out of the evil stored up in his heart. For out of the overflow of his heart his mouth speaks."
~Luke 6:45

We read today's chapter verse, and a visual image materializes of the crowd following Jesus, mesmerized by His words. As it was for them then, it is for us today. Though He's not physically present with us, His wisdom and truth, simple in its expression, capture us in the scriptures; and we too are haunted by its relevance for our present age.

Jesus knows us. Did not God say to Him, *"Let us make mankind in our image, in our likeness...."*? (Genesis 1:26) As our co-creator, He is aware of what goes on within us; and whether it aligns with what we express or demonstrate externally. In other words, God knows the real you and the real me, and what abides out of sight within our heart. This teaching reminds us that within the recess of the heart, good and evil compete for dominance. One of them will thrive; the other will wither. Because the conflict rages internally, God allows us to discern the victor through the mouth, a bodily organ with various functions; communication being a primary one. The words that issue forth reveal our attitudes, our motivations, our beliefs. The actions we do or do not take, our practices or lack thereof, the plans we implement or neglect—all give credence to what the storehouse of our hearts contain. Are its shelves stacked to overflow with loaves of love, jars of joy, parcels of peace, packages of patience, kettles of kindness, gourds of goodness, flasks of faithfulness, gallons of gentleness, sacks of self-control? When the bounty it contains is good, what spills out will give witness. And it goes without saying that good's opposite—evil—will reveal wares that are contrary to what good stores.

O, Lord, what are we to do? We struggle to control our tongues and avoid saying the wrong thing or hiding the truth. The chapter verse words are meant to refocus our efforts. The real culprit is what resides within the heart. There is where the battle wages and must be won.

Prayer: Father God, help us win this battle. Without your guidance and strength, we are lost. Daily, create in our hearts purity and desires that reflect your will. Forgive us for our sins. In Jesus' name. Amen.

Reflection: On a scale of one to ten, where do you rank yourself in a heart assessment that measures the content of your heart as judged by your words and actions? Take some time to meditate and then respond in the space below.

Faith Response:

HUSH!

"Why do you call me, 'Lord, Lord,' and do not do what I say? I will show you what he is like who comes to me and hears my words and puts them into practice."

~Luke 6:46–47

Jesus taught knowing that what He spoke needed to be meaningful to those in His immediate hearing and for those in generations yet unborn. He achieved that goal. His lessons were timely then and they remain so today. Following His rather direct accusation that many who fawned over Him, calling Him 'Lord' were false worshippers (to His face calling Him 'Lord,' and behind His back ignoring what He said), He proceeded to spell out what obedience to Him should look like. One need not be a Rhodes Scholar to get His point. Obedience to God was akin to constructing a house on rock to withstand the storms that were sure to come against it; whereas disobedience to God was like a man who built his house on sand with the inevitable result of it being washed away for lack of a solid foundation. The house built upon the rock obviously stood after the storm, whereas the one constructed on sand did not. If surviving life's storms or challenges is our goal, we must be obedient.

Obedience is not static. It's a noun that requires action to manifest itself. When we claim God as our Lord, the assertion will reflect itself in what we do. Ergo, our obedience to Him is demonstrated by whether we are living in His image and are obedient to His commands recorded in the scriptures. Simple really. Half the battle will be won if we can manage to obey just the two commandments

Jesus said were the greatest of all: to love God with all our heart, mind and soul; and our neighbor as ourselves. Stands to reason in my mind anyway, that the behavior of those who profess the Christian faith should be recognizable in their adherence to at least these foundational principles of that faith. Only then will saluations, cries and shouts of "Lord, Lord" have validity. Otherwise, God's calling out then has not faded. Like a bell, it tolls the same truth today.

Prayer: Father God, it's almost too easy to present oneself as a person of faith. We wear well the outer images that suggest we are and oh, how enthusiastic we are when calling your name in worship! Onlookers can be excused for thinking that surely, we are people of God. But You know our hearts. And You give witness to our thoughts. Forgive us for the incongruity therein. Help us mature in our faith practices such that what we proclaim aligns with what we do in obedience to your word. In Jesus' name we pray. Amen.

Reflection: On which side of the coin do you see yourself? Does God see you? If steps need to be taken for you to be on the same page with Jesus, what are they? Will you commit to correction? Reflect and pray as you are led. Respond in the section below.

Faith Response:

HUSH!

"Where is your faith?" He asked His disciples.

~Luke 8:25

The back story to the question Jesus asked his disciples is a familiar one to many. At some point in His itinerant ministry, He expressed a desire to go over to the other side of Lake Galilee. Before they arrived at their destination, as Jesus slept, a storm arose, and the boat was swamped. The terrified disciples awakened Him and after He calmed the squall with a verbal rebuke, He posed the question, even as we might assume He already knew the answer. Their faith or the exercise of their faith was where it is for most of us when unexpected storms arise and rage across the landscape of our lives.

In the initial moments of trouble, fear, or desperation, our faith slips into its magician's cape and disappears behind the curtain. Left naked and unprotected by the onslaught of whatever the peril of the moment, we do what the frightened disciples did. We cry out to God, with whispers of "Sweet Jesus, help me."

Notice the sequence of events that transpired before Jesus dealt with the emergency. He could have awakened, espied the scene, heard the wailing of his followers, chastised them with His question, and then quelched the squall with the verbal rebuke that quieted the wind and raging sea waters. Instead, He brought order to the chaos first and addressed the faith issue after quietness settled upon the sea.

Did Jesus' timing have a hidden purpose? Would the disciples' awe and amazement of His power have been the same if He had chastised them first for their lack of faith? Would their focus have shifted from His divinity to the shame of the weakness of their faith? We have no way of knowing, as the next account recorded by Luke is unrelated. We are left to ponder the question, *Was there a lesson for us in the timing of Jesus' actions?*

Perhaps the takeaway is that faith can be dormant (temporarily inactive or inoperative) when there are no challenges, no dangers, no dire diagnoses that confront us. But when the storms do arise, dormant faith must be activated. In the moments of danger, confusion, etc., Jesus expects our faith to meet Him on the battlefield, so to speak, with praises of His power before it even manifests. Yes, He will fight our battle and carry the day, but our faith in Him ought to be so overwhelming that nothing He brings to pass astonishes us. After all, He is God. Of course, He controls the outcomes and declares the victor. Repeat after me, "HE IS GOD!" Our hope is built on nothing less than that reality.

Prayer: Father God, our faith can be inconsistent. We proclaim it loudly at a moment's notice when life is smooth sailing. But, when it's not, our faith is prone to vacillate. Today, we pray for faith consistency and for faith that begins praising You for the victory before You enter the fray. In Jesus' name. Amen.

Reflection: Go down memory lane. Have you had "faith drops," before? You know, those times when things were so awful, doubt broke through and overshadowed faith? At what level is your faith now – in the top ten percent or wavering whenever trouble arises? Reflect, meditate, and respond as you are led in the spaces below.

Faith Response:

HUSH!

He said to another man, "Follow me." But he replied, "Lord, first let me go and bury my father." Jesus said to him, "Let the dead bury their own dead, but you go and proclaim the kingdom of God."
~Luke 9:59–60

Jesus' response to a man to whom He had invited to follow Him seems rather callous. It wasn't like the man had said, "*No, I don't want to follow you.*" He explained he needed a little time before he could because of the urgent family business. Then, he'd be "*all in*" as the saying goes. Not alluding to wanting bereavement time to grieve the loss of his father might further suggest that he did want to join the Jesus movement. But our Lord was abruptly clear. Or as I take the liberty to paraphrase, "I need you to be about taking care of my mission not yours.

A natural question for us is what prompted Jesus to respond as He did. Did He perceive something the text did not express? Was the man's answer just an excuse, a way out of making a commitment? We don't know as the passage leaves us clueless. But if we factor in God's purposes for Jesus' time on earth, a reason for Jesus' abruptness becomes clearer. Jesus was "on the clock" so to speak. He had no earthly retirement plan in His portfolio. His stay here was limited. He had no time for bantering or back and forth exchanges. It was imperative that those He asked to spread His teachings and commandments when He was no longer physically with them be dedicated without compromise. That kind of commitment meant cultural norms would often fall by the wayside for whoever signed on, who committed to go and *"proclaim the kingdom of God."* No, Jesus' response wasn't one of callousness but of urgency. *Before long, the world will not see me anymore, ..."* (John 14:19)

The chapter verse speaks to us today with that same urgency, especially if we are among those professing to be Christ followers. The mission Jesus set in motion is well beyond its nascent stage. The Christian faith ranks as the most prominent religion with approximately 2.4 billion followers throughout the world. But numbers don't equate to obedience to the faith professed. Too many Christians are like the prospective follower in the referenced scripture. Though we've signed on to "proclaim the kingdom" by our acceptance of Christ and becoming members of the community of faith (the church), we make excuses, not of taking care of other duties first, but lack of obedience to the very precepts we proclaim. We fail to live the faith we profess, often because the teachings are outside the secular societal norms that we adhere to. The proclamation of God's kingdom is dormant unless it is acted upon. We give excuses to avoid the conflict inherent in being in the world without being of the world. It's a difficult undertaking in a world in which secular pursuits and interests dominate. Daily we must choose to not just proclaim we are Christians, but to give witness to the proclamation in thought, word and deed; to give life to what we proclaim despite the sacrifices doing so may require.

Prayer: Father God, my prayer is simple. Help me daily to live what I profess. When I stumble, help me up and refocus me. In Jesus' name. Amen.

Reflection: Meditate upon your faith in the moment. Do you just proclaim it or do you live it? Is your witness authentic or just for show? Record your thoughts in the spaces below.

Reflection Response:

HUSH!

Someone asked, "Lord, are only a few people going to be saved?"
He said to them, "Make every effort to enter through the narrow
door because, many I tell you, will try to enter and will not be able to.
… But he will answer, 'I don't know you or where you come from.'"
~Luke 13:23–25

As Jesus made His way toward Jerusalem, He continued His teachings and miraculous acts, speaking of current issues and the sinfulness that abounded in the time in which they lived. He urged them to repent or perish. At one point, someone in the crowd asked the question referred to in today's scripture. It was not a question out of the ordinary. Many were probably wondering about the same thing. Jesus deflected the question. How many was not the issue to be concerned about. Whether many or few, the important question was what "i's" had to be dotted, and "t's" crossed to enter a gate that in its narrowness would admit a limited number?

Jesus gave no specifics regarding the narrow door other than a parable of liking it to someone knocking on a door and the owner of said house refusing them entrance with the response: *"I don't know you or where you come from."* (Luke 13:25) We assume that He meant entrance to the narrow door was reserved for those who had in faith accepted Him as being who He said He was, the Son of God, the heralded Messiah; and who had obeyed His teachings and commandments. Given mankind's natural propensity for sin and disobedience, that would not be many because when they knocked, the proprietor would refuse to open it because he didn't know who they were. If anyone was to enter, they must have successfully completed the visa requirements before approaching the gate.

To have done that meant they had made choices along the way whether to adhere to God's word or the word of the world. It would be those of the latter choice who spent their lives tweaking God's teachings to follow the secular. They would be the ones who chose to straddle the divide, and thereby blurring their identity. Unlike them those who knew God and lived in His image will reach the narrow door of eternity's entrance. As they approach, God will smile and say, "I know you, Welcome." And they will enter.

Prayer: Father God, your words are so real. What excuse can we give for disobedience? None! Yet, we stray anyway. In our humanness, forgive us and redirect us so that we mature in obedience. In Jesus name. Amen.

Reflection: Examine your faith journey to date. Are you walking the path leading to the narrow door or the wider one? Is there yet room for redirection, refocus? Respond in the space below.

Faith Response:

HUSH!

"Let any one of you who is without sin be the first to throw a stone at her."

~John 8:7

In one of the most poignant accounts of Jesus' ministry He reveals in this passage a fundamental principal of the gospel message. He spoke the words noted above to the men who had brought to Him for condemnation and stoning (common in that time) a woman caught in the act of adultery. Students of the Bible are familiar with the account, I'm sure. It has always puzzled me why her co-transgressor wasn't hauled alongside her before the Lord (it did take two for that tango), but we'll leave that discussion for another day. Listening in silence as the crowd pontificated her transgression and seeking to accuse Him of not obeying the law, Jesus waited and began to write with his finger on the ground before Him. Only once did He appear to acknowledge the group and that was when He spoke the words above. Then He continued writing until one by one the accusers began leaving. What Jesus wrote on the ground remains a biblical mystery. What He said to the finger-pointers of the woman's sin remains a hallmark of our faith witness today.

It's significant that Jesus did not ignore the sin that had been committed. She was in the wrong. But His words to her reveal His nature and its relevance for us. In contemporary speak, He says, *"What you did was wrong. Cease from that behavior and obey the law. No one condemned you; neither do I. You are forgiven."* God's reason for allowing Jesus to die for our sins paved the way for our redemption.

All have sinned and come short of God's glory, but we are forgiven because of Jesus' sacrifice that covered our sins.

As Jesus did with the woman who violated the law, He still does for us today; and as importantly expects us to do unto each another. Yes, the times are vastly different, contemporary wrongs beyond belief. And yes, wrongdoers should be held accountable for their actions. But, and it's a big "But," there is only one Judge, one God to whom all will give account of their sins. Not one of us will be able to claim that we are "without sin." Since sin is synonymous with humanity, perhaps our attention should focus more on the things we struggle to correct, forgive others as God forgives us, and leave the rest to the Lord.

Prayer: Father God, judging others is so easy for us. We are expert at pointing out flaws in those we know and those we just hear about. Accusing words roll off our tongues without hesitancy. Stopping to think about our own sins is often the last thing we do. Maybe on Communion Sundays we remember; maybe not. We ask for forgiveness, Lord, and for the Holy Spirit to control our thoughts and words of condemnation of others. Fill us with a forgiving spirit, the kind that You demonstrate toward us each day. In Jesus' name. Amen.

Reflections: Meditate during your quiet time with Jesus on how this devotional speaks to you. Do you feel convicted? What factors cause you to make the judgments you make against others? On a scale of one to five with five being an indicator that you are "without sin," rank yourself. Ponder why you feel that way. Pray. Respond in the space provided.

Faith Response:

HUSH!

To the Jews who had believed in him, Jesus said, "If you hold to my teaching, you are really my disciples. Then you will know the truth, and the truth will set you free."

~John 8:31–32

That Jesus' earthly ethnicity is Jewish is well established. In His human form, He was born and grew to manhood within the norms of the prevailing Jewish customs, laws and traditions. His features would have been typical of those who lived in the Middle East during His time which suggest that from a racial perspective He was neither Black nor White (as those racial identifiers are termed in the present). In this passage He is talking to people who had made a major decision in their spiritual lives when they accepted this contemporary of theirs to be who He said He was, the long-awaited Son of God. Turning from what they'd been taught and probably adhered to required incredible fortitude and faith. Jesus' promise to them was simple. Holding fast to what He taught would identify them as His true believers. Their allegiance would free them from the ungodliness that kept them in bondage, slaves to the desires of the flesh. Only the truth He taught had the power to free them.

The segue to our time is easy. Many profess to believe in Jesus. They profess Christianity as their religious preference. But beyond those initial steps, many—judging by the moral fiber of the times—still struggle to "hold to" His teachings. To "hold to" in the context in which Jesus spoke means to abide by, follow, live up, embrace, adhere to. As I've noted before, sometimes modern day "disciples" are hard to spot. They blend secular norms that contradict Jesus' teachings into the faith practices He taught. They wear the trappings of faith, not realizing that in so doing they remain slaves to the sin from which Jesus' teachings are designed to free them.

God's word still provides the only roadmap to eternity. There may be various translations of it, but its essence is immutable. Truth abides therein. As surely as modern-day communication satellites give direction and guidance to a host of secular things, the Bible gives the same to those in pursuit of freedom from sin and eternal life. Throw off those trappings and *"seek the Lord while He may be found."* Grasp His truth and be free.

Prayer: Father God, too often your truth eludes us because we do not obey your teachings. We give lip service; the truth buried beneath the secular's attractions. Help us, Lord. Forgive us. Set us right. In Jesus' name we pray. Amen.

Reflection: Meditate quietly as the His words speak to you. Can you say "Amen" and mean it? Respond to the devotional in the space provided below.

Reflection Response:

HUSH!

As he went along, he saw a man blind from birth. His disciples asked him, "Rabbi, who sinned, this man or his parents, that he was born blind?"

"Neither this man nor his parents sinned," said Jesus, "but this happened so that the work of God might be displayed in his life."

~John 9:1–3

Societal misconceptions about physical abnormalities are nothing new. They held sway within the general community in Jesus' time as some do today. In the 21st century despite scientific knowledge that was obviously absent during the 1st, individuals with physical disabilities are perceived as, according to "Centre Disability Support," among other things a "*burden on society, all the same, are victims, are defined by their disability*, etc." In Jesus time, such conditions were summed up in the common belief that they were the result of sin. Or as we might say in the vernacular of the day, "*Somebody sinned for that to have happened.*" The disciples assumed as much and wanted to know who—the parents or the baby itself (remember he was born blind). Jesus cut through the nonsense. The issue was not "sin." The issue was what God intended to do through the disability. Jesus proceeded to heal the man of his sightlessness, and in so doing demonstrated the power God has over all of life.

What can we take away from this account of another of Jesus' miracles? It reminds us of whom it is we serve. Despite our suffering: infirmities, disabilities—mental and physical, God has not forsaken His beloved. He is at His best when He ministers to us as we struggle with these shortcomings. We come to understand that faith without testing is not faith at all. The world we reside in is anything but perfect. We are puzzled when good people suffer, and their opposites prosper. As we pray and wait, God rewards us with His comfort and peace; anxiety lessens, and joy takes up residence into the spaces it leaves behind. The man who was healed said it best, *"One thing I know. I was blind but now I see."* We can echo that praise. Whether healed of our diseases, the physical, mental or emotional challenges we face daily or continuing to live with them, one thing we know. Once we were lost and now, we are found. No, the world isn't fair. But the God we serve holds the upper hand. He plays it to achieve His purposes. They are for our good and His glory. We accept that and know the peace of His presence.

Prayer: Father God, when life's challenges confound us and we struggle handling its disparities, come in those moments of confusion and doubt. Reveal yourself to us through the Holy Spirit and just the right scripture for that moment. We seek your healing, a normal life free of disabling issues. But more than that, we want what You've wanted for us since our birth. Whatever that looks like, may your peace be sufficient. In Jesus' name. Amen.

Reflection: Do you struggle with unresolved issues over which you've prayed for release and are still waiting? Does the piece help you in coming to peace while continuing to wait? How so? Respond as you are led in the space provided below.

Reflection Response:

HUSH!

"Peace I leave with you; my peace I give you. I do not give to you as the world gives. Do not let your hearts be troubled and do not be afraid."

~John14:27

Just before Jesus spoke these words to the disciples, He said that God would send the Holy Spirit to serve as a Counselor who would continue His teachings and remind them of all He'd said. In essence it was to be through the Holy Spirit that the peace He was leaving would be activated. That it was to come from a divine source rather than a secular one, the peace of which He spoke would be unlike what "peace" was generally thought to be.

Then as now, we associate the term peace to mean an absence of conflict. And for the most part from a secular perspective it is. Peace between individuals or groups implies for both that whatever disagreements kept them at each other's throats would disappear. Reconciliation would lay to rest the conflicting elements.

But Jesus was clear. The peace they were to receive from Him would not be within the framework of the ordinary. As they would come to know, and today we can testify to, Jesus' peace is extraordinary because of what does in and for us. It is an internal transformation, not an external event. The forces of sin, fear, uncertainty, and doubt that wage war within us are laid to rest with Jesus' peace which He gives when we accept Him as our Savior and obey His teachings. We view even our external conflicts or challenges through the lens of that peace.

If we the remove the place cards of *worry* and *anxiety* from our table and replace them with those of *prayer*, *petition*, and *thanksgiving*, we will find to be true the words Philippians 4:6–7 proclaim: *"the peace of God, which transcends all understanding, will guard our hearts and minds in Christ Jesus."* At that point there will be no reason for disquieted hearts or fearful spirits. Let hurricanes, floods, earthquakes, fires, tsunamis, crime, political upheaval, illness, death, wars and rumors of war come—none of these devastating misfortunes or tragedies—will stand against or prevent Jesus' peace from fulfilling the purposes for which He gives it.

Prayer: Father God, though we know these words to be our truth as believers, still we struggle to live as if we believe them. Mature our faith; heighten our trust and create daily in us hearts and minds with greater obedience to your Word by living as if we believe them. In Jesus' name. Amen.

Reflections: How would you rate yourself in living as if Jesus' peace is rock solid in your life? Are there areas in which you still struggle? Respond in the spaces below.

Faith Response:

HUSH!

"Remain in me and I will remain in you. … If a man remains in me and I in him, he will bear much fruit; apart from me you can do nothing."

~John 1:4–5

Jesus speaks what we may term "parting remarks" as He approaches the climax of His earthly mission. It has been three years of ministering and teaching the motley crew He called disciples. The verses above capture the crucial element of His teachings if they were to bear fruit and succeed. The disciples, and others who would come to accept Jesus as Savior, had to stay connected to Him as a fruitful branch remains connected to its source of nourishment. The lessons He'd intoned would die "on the vine" if they lost their connection to Jesus. And the only way they had of doing that was to "remain" in Him and He in them. "Remaining" in Jesus meant they would preach and teach Jesus as the Son of God, claim Him as their Savior and Lord, obey the message of the gospel He espoused and adhere to the two commandments He stated were the greatest: loving God with our total being and loving our neighbor (stranger) as ourselves. If they lost their connection to Him, none of their labor would succeed.

Once again, we can marvel at the wonder of the gospel, and its unending relevance across two thousand years. Jesus knew that in 2025 we of the Christian faith need to hear this caution. Repeatedly, perhaps even more than those who were eyewitnesses, we need to be reminded of what our faith walk ought to look like if we remain in

Jesus and He in us. Sadly, our portrait too often bears little resemblance to the Lord's word, primarily because one pesky precept keeps tripping us, and breaks the connection. "Obedience."

Obeying the gospel message takes a back seat to the "showing" of the gospel. Perhaps that's why, despite the billions of professed Christians, the plethora of churches, the parade of preachers, evangelists, teachers, workers, praise choirs, musicians, biblical curriculums, annual convocations and conferences, prayer meetings, retreats, and a host of other displays of faith, sin prevails. A quote by Oswald Chambers kind of sums it up. "Christianity is character, not 'show business.'" If one's internal being does not remain in Jesus, submissive to His will, the connection to Him frays over time. He remains in place, but we "pull the plug" so to speak by our disobedience, preventing us from bearing the fruit He desires, not what we decide He desires. He has told us what He requires of us. But we prefer our way; and continue to wonder why we don't flourish. Why we do not bear fruit.

Prayer: Father God, forgive us. Help us be doers of your word and not just hearers. Bring us back into relationship with You via our connection to Jesus and the Holy Word. Give us an obedient spirit and heart. In Jesus' name. Amen.

Reflections: What were your take-aways from this devotional? Do you agree or disagree with the with the commentary's statement: "Christianity is character, not show business"? Share your thoughts in the space provided.

Faith Response:

HUSH!

Then Jesus came to them and said, "All authority in heaven and earth has been given to me. Therefore, go and make disciples of all nations, baptizing them in the name of the Father and of the Son and of the Holy Spirit, and teaching them to obey everything I have commanded you. And surely, I am with you always, to the very end of the age."

~Matthew 28:18–20

*O*nly the gospel of Matthew records these words of the Savior. Termed Jesus' "Great Commission," this farewell address became the "lynchpin" of the Christian faith. What He spoke guided the disciples and emerging apostles as they carried them far beyond Jerusalem. Those nascent missionaries of the good news crossed racial, ethnic and regional lines as they brought Jesus' message to whomever had ears to hear.

This final in person address was not however a "retirement" speech. Not even close. Jesus made it clear that though He would no longer physically "*be in the office*" every day, the authority which would guide God's mission still rested with Him. He would always be with them in spirit, as He had earlier told them. The internal Holy Spirit, we might say, would be Jesus' "*boots on the ground.*" Guided by it, Jesus' disciples labored in the ensuing years, bringing many to harvest.

The work of those disciples who watched as Jesus ascended back into Heaven and those who followed them continues in this 21st century. Yes, these two thousand and counting years later, Jesus' commission stands. And though the church may have codified it within the framework of denominational structures, the essence of what Jesus commanded them to do remains. Whether clergy or laity, followers of Jesus are charged to share the word of God. And though some sacraments, baptizing and communion among them, fall under the auspices of the clergy, all who profess the name of Christ are called to "teach", i.e. show by example and model what He taught. We are called to "go"—to imitate Christ in our lifestyles—next door, in line at the grocery store, waiting in the doctor's office, to be wherever Jesus, working through the Holy Spirit prompts us to be. Christianity is not an "*I got mine; you get yours*" way of thinking but rather a "*Here's what I've got; I'd like to share it with you*" belief mode. When we live with the latter kind of attitude, Jesus' Spirit reflects itself in us. And who knows? Those who have ears to hear may be moved to follow. That is our everlasting hope.

Prayer: Father God, the accounts of Jesus' time on earth never grow old. Each rereading of them brings joy, comfort and hope to all who believe and wait for His second coming. As we do, keep us focused on what your word commands. Help us live exemplary lives of discipleship such that others are curious and want to know what gives us such peace in unpeaceful times. We pray in His name. Amen.

Reflections: Are you living in ways that others identify you easily as a disciple of Jesus, not just someone who goes to church on Sunday? What about your lifestyle or attitude needs adjustment or refocusing? Pray to Jesus to help you through His Spirit to realign your practices with His teachings. Share your thoughts in the space below.

Faith Reflection:

Final Word

"Behold, I am coming soon. My reward is with me, and I will give to everyone according to what he has done. I am the Alpha and the Omega, the First and the Last, the Beginning and the End."

~Revelation 22:12–13

Acknowledgements

Trust in the Lord with all your heart and lean not on your own understanding; in all your ways acknowledge him and he will make your path straight.

~Proverbs 3:5–6

Giving honor and glory to God, I am grateful once again for the leading of His Spirit in the crafting of my 8th devotional book. With the Holy Spirit as my Muse and the Holy Word as my source document, the explications came to life. As with all my writing, the purpose is unchanged. My desire and hope are that others are drawn to Jesus, accept Him as their personal Savior and become His disciples.

Once again, I am grateful to and thankful for Ann Lloyd, ("my sister by another mother," aka Sbam) who continues to serve as my "critical ear," listening for biblical blunders and offering suggestions to enhance a particular theme. My first drafts would be halted at the gate if not for her editing support.

Thank you to my immediate and extended family as well as friends and friends of friends who support my efforts, and offer encouragement Many buy books to read and to share with others.

My journey continues filled with the joys and surprises that only grandchildren bring. One of them this year was the birth of my first great grandchild, Zymir. He joins the "Grand 4" (now the "Grand 4 + 1"): Logan, Jordan (Zymir's dad), Brooklin and Quentin KE. As is my refrain, "They are God's gifts that keep on giving." It is a blessing indeed to be their Nyanya.

My usual shout-out to my editor and publisher Mike Parker at Wordcraft Press. I consider him a partner in my efforts and thank him for his ongoing support and encouragement.

Beverly ND Clopton
Mesquite, Texas

About the Author

Beverly ND Clopton is the eldest of nine children. She grew up in Dallas and completed her undergraduate studies in the great state of Texas before she embarked on a 40-year calling as a professional educator in the Dallas, Denver, and Los Angeles public school systems.

Stepping into retirement offered Beverly the opportunity to return to her first loves—the written word and the Word of God.

She has since published numerous books of essays and devotionals, including *Heaven or Bust: Journey to Glory, Sonshine: Reflections of Faith, Surviving Pitfalls on the Path, Rigors of the Call, Until I Die: Reflections and Tales, Lingering in the Word: a 40 Day Devotional,* and *God in the Commonplace.* Beverly's next book, *Any Time—Any Place 365 Days of Reflective Devotionals* is currently "on the potter's wheel."

Also by

Beverly ND Clopton

God in the Commonplace
Lingering in the Word
Until I Die
Rigors of the Call
Sonshine: Reflections of Faith
Surviving Pitfalls on the Path
Heaven or Bust: Journey to Glory

Aslo Available from
WordCrafts Press

Free Indeed
Dr. Brian C. Johnson

Illuminations
by Paula K. Parker

Morning Mist
by Barbie Loflin

The Gift of Peace
by Kira McCullough & Keb Burns

www.wordcrafts.net